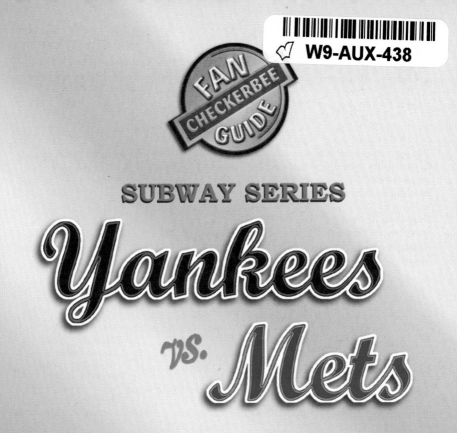

FAN CHECKERBEE GUIDE

SUBWAY SERIES

Yankees

vs. Mets

Commemorative Edition

The New York Mets, led by manager Bobby Valentine (left), faced off against
the New York Yankees, led by manager Joe Torre (right), in the 2000 World Series.

Subway Series
Yankees vs. Mets

*This book is dedicated to the late Murry Davis and all the great fans who
dreamed of a Subway Series between the Yankees and the Mets.*

This publication is not affiliated with the New York Yankees, the New York Mets, Major League
Baseball or any of its affiliates, subsidiaries, distributors or representatives. Any opinions expressed
are solely those of the authors, and do not necessarily reflect those of the New York Yankees, the New
York Mets or Major League Baseball.

Front Cover (left to right): Yogi Berra embraces Don Larsen after Larsen pitched a perfect game in
Game 5 of the 1956 World Series (AP/WWP); Benny Agbayani congratulates Robin Ventura after
Ventura hit a home run in Game 3 of the 2000 World Series (AP/WWP); Yankee players mob Jose
Vizcaino after his game-winning hit in Game 1 of the 2000 World Series (AP/WWP).

	EDITORIAL		**ART**
Managing Editor:	Jeff Mahony	Creative Director:	Joe T. Nguyen
Associate Editors:	Melissa A. Bennett	Assistant Art Director:	Lance Doyle
	Jan Cronan	Senior Graphic Designers:	Marla B. Gladstone
	Gia C. Manalio		Susannah C. Judd
	Mike Micciulla		David S. Maloney
	Paula Stuckart		Carole Mattia-Slater
Assistant Editors:	Heather N. Carreiro		David Ten Eyck
	Jennifer Renk	Graphic Designers:	Jennifer J. Bennett
	Joan C. Wheal		Sean-Ryan Dudley
Editorial Assistants:	Timothy R. Affleck		Kimberly Eastman
	Beth Hackett		Melani Gonzalez
	Christina M. Sette		Caryn Johnson
	Steven Shinkaruk		Jaime Josephiac
			Jim MacLeod
	WEB		Jeremy Maendel
	(CollectorsQuest.com)		Chery-Ann Poudrier
Web Reporter:	Samantha Bouffard		
Web Graphic Designer:	Ryan Falis		**R&D**
		Product Development	
	PRODUCTION	Manager:	Paul Rasid
Production Manager:	Scott Sierakowski	R&D Specialist:	Priscilla Berthiaume

ISBN 1-58598-139-7

CheckerBee
PUBLISHING

306 Industrial Park Road
Middletown, CT 06457

CollectorsQuest
.com

Table Of
Contents

Introducing The CheckerBee Fan Guide™

The 2000 baseball postseason was filled with wonderful memories for the fans of the Yankees and Mets. The Yankees went into the World Series with nearly a century of baseball history and an unbelievable 25 world championships, while the Mets had been around for almost 40 years and had taken baseball's top prize twice. Now, for the first time in history, they would go head-to-head in the World Series for the bragging rights of baseball and, perhaps more importantly, the bragging rights of the Big Apple.

The CheckerBee Fan Guide™ will recount all of the exciting action from the 2000 Subway Series, including the post-series victory parade. Then it's on to stories from die-hard Yankees and Mets fans about their favorite team.

After a look at past Subway Series matchups and a visit to New York ballparks (some of which no longer exist), you will slide in head-first into the lore of each team, from a 2000 season recap and a look at the 2000 players to a decade-by-decade history of each franchise. Then it's on to the souvenir shop where we'll showcase memorabilia from almost a century of New York baseball.

And if you think this covers all bases, keep reading for more!

- A recap of the 2000 Subway Series, including game photos
- Full-color photos of 2000 Subway Series memorabilia
- A showcase of official Yankees and Mets merchandise
- An overview of past Subway Series and New York baseball memorabilia, along with secondary market values
- A look at some of the greatest players and moments in Yankees and Mets history

Game 1
The Longest Game

Derek Jeter congratulates Jose Vizcaino on his game-winning hit.

Saturday, October 21, 2000, Yankee Stadium. It felt more like early summer than late October in the Bronx as the first game of the 2000 Subway Series drew near. The city of New York had been bursting with energy since New Yorkers learned that their dreams of a Subway Series would be a reality. Brother versus brother. Yankees versus Mets. It would be a neighborhood brawl, only televised.

The early evening air surged with excitement, anticipation, aggression, fear. As native New Yorker Billy Joel stepped onto the storied Yankee Stadium turf to sing the national anthem and a bald eagle prepared to soar from beyond the outfield fence towards the pitcher's mound, the crowd stood and cheered with a mixture of city pride and national patriotism.

The raucous ovation of the crowd at the conclusion of the national anthem was starkly contrasted to the somber moment of silence that followed for the young sailors of the United States Navy who perished during the attack on the U.S.S. Cole in Yemen.

Who better to throw out the ceremonial first pitch than Yankee greats Don Larsen and Yogi Berra? In the last Subway Series to descend upon the city, the pitcher-and-catcher combination had participated in the only perfect game in World Series history.

Billy Joel sings the national anthem before Game 1.

Play Ball!

The Game 1 lineup featured some surprises and fans from Montauk to Albany were anxious to find out which manager's moves would pay off. As the game was played in an American League park, Mets manager Bobby Valentine put regular catcher Mike Piazza in the lineup as the designated hitter and put backup catcher Todd Pratt behind the

Yogi Berra and Don Larsen after throwing out the ceremonial first pitch.

plate. Yankees manager Joe Torre placed utility infielder Jose Vizcaino at second base. Vizcaino had a 10-for-19 lifetime hitting record against the Mets' starting pitcher Al Leiter, and Torre wanted to go with the experience.

The game remained scoreless through five innings, with Leiter and the Yankees' Andy Pettitte pitching well. The Yankees were the first ones on the scoreboard when left fielder David Justice belted a double in the bottom of the sixth inning that scored designated hitter Chuck Knoblauch and shortstop Derek Jeter.

But the Mets came right back in the top of the seventh when pinch hitter Bubba Trammell hit a bases loaded, one-out single that scored left fielder Benny Agbayani and center fielder Jay Payton. The next batter sacrificed to advance the runners to second and third, and chased

Pettitte from the game. Right hander Jeff Nelson came in from the bullpen, but Edgardo Alfonzo hit an infield dribbler that scored a run, giving the Mets a 3-2 lead.

The score was still the same when the bottom of the ninth rolled around and Mets' closer Armando Benitez, who had a club-record 41 saves during the regular season, was on the mound. But Benitez, as he had throughout his postseason career, would struggle against his opponents.

Mets pinch hitter Bubba Trammell drives in two runs in the seventh inning.

Right fielder Paul O'Neill battled Benitez for a walk with a gritty 10-pitch at bat. Pinch hitter Luis Polonia ripped a single and surprise starter Vizcaino followed with a single to load the bases. Knoblauch stepped up and smacked a sacrifice fly to score O'Neill and tie the game at 3 runs apiece.

On To Extra Innings!

The Yankees had a chance to end the game in the 10th, but O'Neill hit into a rally-killing double play to end the inning. Then, in the 12th inning, it looked like the Yankees might squander another opportunity. With the bases loaded and two out against Mets' pitcher

Chuck Knoblauch's sacrifice fly ties up the game in the bottom of the ninth.

Turk Wendell, up stepped #9 hitter Vizcaino. He promptly smacked a single to left to drive home first baseman Tino Martinez with the winning run.

Kurt Abbott completes a key double play in the 10th as Posada slides into second.

The Yankees had come from behind to win the game 4-3 in the longest game in World Series history at 4 hours, 51 minutes. And Jose Vizcaino, in his first-ever World Series game, was the unlikely hero. The victory was the Yankees' 13th consecutive World Series win, breaking the 12-game win streak record held by the great Yankees teams of old. It was now the wee hours of Sunday morning, and the two teams would meet again later that day in Game 2.

GAME 1: Yankees 4, Mets 3

METS	AB	R	H	BI	BB	SO	AVG
Perez rf	6	0	1	0	0	1	.167
Alfonzo 2b	6	0	1	1	0	2	.167
Piazza dh	5	0	1	0	0	1	.200
Zeile 1b	5	0	2	0	0	1	.400
Ventura 3b	5	0	0	0	0	1	.000
Agbayani lf	4	1	2	0	0	1	.500
McEwing lf	1	0	0	0	0	0	.000
Payton cf	5	1	1	0	0	0	.200
Pratt c	2	1	0	0	1	2	.000
Bordick ss	1	0	0	0	0	1	.000
Trammell ph	1	0	1	2	0	0	1.000
KAbbott ss	2	0	1	0	0	0	.500
Totals	43	3	10	3	1	10	

YANKEES	AB	R	H	BI	BB	SO	AVG
Knoblauch dh	4	1	0	1	1	1	.000
Jeter ss	4	1	1	0	2	2	.250
Justice lf	4	0	1	2	1	0	.250
Bellinger pr-lf	0	0	0	0	0	0	—
GHill ph-lf	1	0	0	0	0	0	.000
BeWilliams cf	4	0	0	0	2	1	.000
TMartinez 1b	6	1	2	0	0	1	.333
Posada c	5	0	1	0	1	1	.200
O'Neill rf	4	1	1	0	2	1	.250
Brosius 3b	3	0	1	0	0	0	.333
Polonia ph	1	0	1	0	0	0	1.000
Sojo 3b	2	0	0	0	0	0	.000
JVizcaino 2b	6	0	4	1	0	1	.667
Totals	44	4	12	4	9	8	

METS					
METS	000	000	300	000—3	10 0
YANKEES	000	002	001	001—4	12 0

Two outs when winning run scored. **LOB**—Mets 8, Yankees 15. **2B**—Zeile (1), Agbayani (1), KAbbott (1), Justice (1), Posada (1). **RBI**—Alfonzo (1), Trammell 2 (2), Knoblauch (1), Justice 2 (2), JVizcaino (1). **CS**—Piazza (1), Knoblauch (1). **S**—Bordick. **SF**—Knoblauch. **DP**—New York 1.

METS	IP	H	R	ER	BB	SO	NP	ERA
ALeiter	7	5	2	2	3	7	122	2.57
JFranco	1	1	0	0	0	15	0.00	
Benitez	1	2	1	1	1	1	30	9.00
Cook	0	0	0	2	0	9	0.00	
Rusch	1⅓	1	0	0	2	0	21	0.00
Wendell L, 0-1	1	3	1	1	1	0	16	9.00

YANKEES	IP	H	R	ER	BB	SO	NP	ERA
Pettitte	6⅔	8	3	3	1	4	95	4.05
Nelson	1⅓	1	0	0	0	19	0.00	
MRivera	2	1	0	0	3	34	0.00	
Stanton W, 1-0	2	0	0	0	3	23	0.00	

Cook pitched to 2 batters in the 10th. **HBP**—by MRivera (Pratt), by Pettitte (Pratt). **WP**—Rusch 2. **Umpires**—Home, Montague; First, Reliford; Second, Kellogg; Third, Welke, Tim; Left, McClelland; Right, Crawford. **T**—4:51. **A**—55,913 (57,545).

Game 2

Rocket-Propelled!

AP/WWP

Mike Piazza's shattered bat heads toward Roger Clemens.

Sunday, October 22, 2000, Yankee Stadium. For one game only, the Yankees-Mets rivalry took a back seat in the pre-game hype to the personal tension between Mets' hero Mike Piazza and Yankees' pitcher Roger "Rocket" Clemens. In an inter-league game during the regular season, Clemens had hit Piazza on the head with an inside fastball that felled the mighty batter and took him out of the game (and the subsequent All-Star Game) with a concussion. And as the second battle of the boroughs approached, the city of New York braced itself for an electric first-inning reunion between the two foes.

With two outs in the first inning, it was Piazza's turn at the plate. Things were uneventful until Clemens' fourth pitch. Piazza swung, hit a foul ball and instinctively ran down the first baseline. His bat shattered with the impact of the pitch and a piece of it skittered toward Clemens on the mound. Clemens picked up the hunk of splintered and jagged wood and hurled it off the diamond – and directly in the path of the jogging Piazza.

Piazza was shocked, but he remained calm.

Players from both teams rush to the mound after Clemens throws the bat fragment toward Piazza.

Piazza approached Clemens, demanding to know why he threw the bat. The Yankees and Mets benches cleared and the Yankees in the field came to the infield in anticipation of defending their teammates. The umpires rushed in, but were quickly satisfied that Clemens meant no ill will, and called for play to resume. Piazza returned to the batter's box and hit a harmless grounder to end the inning.

Now That That's Over With . . .

The bottom of the first inning brought Mike Hampton to the mound for the Mets. Like Clemens, he retired his first two batters easily. But things got tricky for him after that. He walked the next two batters on eight straight balls. Tino Martinez smacked a single to left field that scored David Justice, and then Bernie Williams scored on a single from Jorge Posada.

Down 2-0 in the first inning and fired up by Clemens' tossed bat, the Mets were eager to come up to bat and show Clemens up.

Tino Martinez hits a single to drive in the first run of the game.

But they didn't. The intense Clemens didn't get rattled by the bizarre first-inning encounter and pitched eight masterful innings,

AP/WWP

toying with the Mets batters. The Rocket racked up nine strikeouts and allowed only two hits, both to Mets first baseman Todd Zeile.

Going into the ninth inning, the Yankees were up 6-0 and it looked like Clemens had propelled the Yanks to an easy Game 2 victory. But with Clemens out of the game, the Mets had one inning left in which to get their retribution. The Mets' first batter, Edgardo Alfonzo, smacked a single off the Yankees' new pitcher Jeff Nelson.

Mike Hampton was the Mets' Game 2 starter.

Piazza came up next and promptly hit a home run to make the score 6-2. Then third baseman Robin Ventura came up and slipped a single through the hole into center.

Yankees manager Joe Torre had seen enough and brought in his ace, Mariano Rivera. He got the first two outs (which included Clay Bellinger's catch at the left-field wall to rob Zeile of a probable home run), but the Mets had put runners at second and third and they weren't ready to go home just yet.

AP/WWP

Roger Clemens maintained his velocity throughout eight strong innings.

Rookie outfielder Jay Payton came to the plate and hit Rivera's third pitch into the right-field stands for a stunning three-run

AP/WWP

home run to bring the Mets within one run of tying the game. But Rivera shook off the Mets' fireworks and struck out Kurt Abbott on a called third strike to end the game.

Looking Ahead

With the Game 2 win, the Yankees set a new record for consecutive World Series wins with 14 and they would head to Shea Stadium

Piazza and Edgardo Alfonzo celebrate the catcher's two-run homer in the ninth.

with a commanding 2-0 Subway Series lead. But the Yankees knew (as well as the Mets) that a 2-0 World Series deficit was not insurmountable, as the Yankees had come back from the same deficit in 1996 against the Atlanta Braves and the Mets had achieved the feat in 1986 against the Boston Red Sox. That being said, the Mets still had to head back to Queens with the fear of becoming the third straight team to be swept in the World Series by the New York Yankees.

Clemens' Plea For Clemency

After the game, Clemens would say that he was responding instinctively: he thought the bat was a foul ball and was tossing it off of the playing field and into the dugout. Yankee Manager Joe Torre defended Clemens endlessly, as did his teammates. The Mets were outraged at Clemens' action and called for a disciplinary review. The next day, Major League Baseball fined the hurler $50,000.

GAME 2: Yankees 6, Mets 5

NEW YORK (N)	AB	R	H	BI	BB	SO	AVG
Perez rf	4	0	0	0	0	1	.100
Alfonzo 2b	3	1	1	0	0	1	.222
Piazza c	4	1	1	2	0	0	.222
Ventura 3b	4	0	1	0	0	1	.111
Zeile 1b	4	0	2	0	0	0	.444
Agbayani lf	4	1	1	0	0	2	.375
LHarris dh	4	1	0	0	0	1	.000
Payton cf	4	1	1	3	0	1	.222
Bordick ss	2	0	0	0	0	1	.000
Hamilton ph	1	0	0	0	0	1	.000
KAbbott ss	1	0	0	0	0	1	.333
Totals	35	5	7	5	0	10	

NEW YORK (A)	AB	R	H	BI	BB	SO	AVG
Knoblauch dh	4	0	0	0	1	0	.000
Jeter ss	5	1	3	0	0	1	.444
Justice lf	3	1	0	0	1	1	.143
Bellinger lf	0	0	0	0	0	0	—
BeWilliams cf	3	1	0	0	2	0	.000
TMartinez 1b	5	1	3	2	0	0	.455
Posada c	3	1	2	1	2	0	.375
O'Neill rf	4	0	3	1	0	1	.500
Brosius 3b	3	1	1	2	0	1	.333
JVizcaino 2b	4	0	0	0	0	1	.400
Totals	34	6	12	6	6	5	

NEW YORK (N)	000	000	005—5	7	3
NEW YORK (A)	210	010	11x—6	12	1

E—Perez (1), Payton (1), Bordick (1), Clemens (1). LOB—New York (N) 4, New York (A) 12. 2B—Jeter 2 (2), TMartinez (1), O'Neill (1). HR—Payton (1) off MRivera; Piazza (1) off Nelson; Brosius (1) off Hampton. RBI—Piazza 2 (2), Payton 3 (3), TMartinez 2 (2), Posada (1), O'Neill (1), Brosius 2 (2). CS—JVizcaino (1). SF—Brosius.

NEW YORK (N)	IP	H	R	ER	BB	SO	NP	ERA
Hampton L, 0-1	6	8	4	4	5	4	120	6.00
Rusch	⅓	2	1	1	0	0	11	4.50
RAWhite	1⅓	1	1	1	1	1	19	6.75
Cook	⅓	1	0	0	0	0	4	0.00
NEW YORK (A)	IP	H	R	ER	BB	SO	NP	ERA
Clemens W, 1-0	8	2	0	0	0	9	112	0.00
Nelson	0	3	3	3	0	0	7	20.25
MRivera	1	2	2	2	0	1	18	6.00

Nelson pitched to 3 batters in the 9th. HBP—by Hampton (Justice), by Clemens (Alfonzo). WP—Clemens. PB—Posada. Umpires—Home, Reliford; First, Kellogg; Second, Welke, Tim; Third, McClelland; Left, Crawford; Right, Montague. T—3:30. A—56,059 (57,545).

Game 3

Invincible No More

Mets manager Bobby Valentine congratulates Benny Agbayani after Game 3.

Tuesday, October 24, 2000, Shea Stadium. The first pitch had yet to be thrown at Shea Stadium in Game 3 of the World Series, but to the armchair coaches and sports radio pundits who obsess over every tiny statistic, the New York Mets were already down three games to none against the New York Yankees.

On paper, things certainly looked grim for the Mets. The Yankees' ace pitcher Orlando "El Duque" Hernandez had eight October wins under his belt and had never lost in the postseason. Hernandez had battled a flu bug just before his Game 3 start, but the Yankees

Orlando Hernandez had won eight consecutive postseason games coming into Game 3.

weren't worried. Opposing hitters hadn't been able to shut down El Duque, so why would the flu?

Rick Reed, working the mound for the Mets on nine days of rest, hadn't started since Game 3 against St. Louis in the National League Championship Series. Reed, who carried an 0-2 lifetime record against the Yankees going into the game, would have to pitch the game of his life to keep the Mets alive.

But a funny thing happened on the way to the sweep.

Refusing to roll over and play dead, the Mets would find heroics from the most unlikely of places and make a fourth October coronation in five years for the Yankees anything but a certainty.

A Pitching Duel

To this point, El Duque had been one of the most imposing pitchers ever to hurl in the postseason, but his penchant for coughing up the long ball was an Achilles' heel. El Duque had given up 34 home runs during the regular season, the third-highest total in the American League. In the bottom of the second inning, Hernandez tossed a no-out pitch to Robin Ventura, who hit it out of the yard. Unfazed by the blast, Hernandez went on to strike out Todd Zeile, Benny Agbayani and Jay Payton to end the inning.

Robin Ventura hits a solo home run in the second inning.

In the top of the third, it was the Yankees' turn to put a run on the board. Derek Jeter got a two-out single that kept alive his 12-game World Series hitting streak. David Justice, the MVP of the American League

Championship Series, scored Jeter with a double, giving Justice his 12th RBI of the postseason.

The Yankees took the lead in the fourth inning after the hot-hitting Tino Martinez led off with a base hit. Jorge Posada struck out, but Paul O'Neill hit his first triple of the year to score Martinez and give the Yankees a 2-1 advantage.

Rick Reed was the Mets' Game 3 starter.

The pitching duel between Hernandez and Reed continued into the bottom of the sixth when things seemed ready to unravel for El Duque. Mike Piazza roped a double down the left field line to lead off the inning. Ventura reached on a walk. Zeile scored Piazza with an RBI double to tie the game, and now the Mets had two runners in scoring position with nobody out as Benny Agbayani stepped to the plate. Agbayani had predicted a Mets championship in five games, and had been eating his words with his every plate appearance. Now he had a chance to bust the game wide open for the Mets. He worked the count full and eventually drew a walk. With the bases loaded and nobody out, Hernandez demonstrated why he was undefeated in October. El Duque recorded back-to-back strikeouts on the next two batters and got the third to ground out to end the inning with no more runners crossing the plate.

Reed left the game and the Mets turned to Game 1 losing pitcher Turk Wendell. An avowed hunter, Wendell wore a menacing necklace made up of the teeth of his various hunting trophies. Wendell's performance was anything but toothless, striking out two before allowing a walk. Wendell was then pulled in favor of southpaw Dennis Cook, who finished the inning.

The Mets and their fans are glad to be back at Shea Stadium.

In the bottom of the eighth with the score tied at 2, Hernandez seemed as fresh as he had in the first inning. He got Ventura to strike out for his 12th strikeout of the game. Zeile, however, stroked a single,

bringing Agbayani back up to the plate. Agbayani slammed a double in the gap in center and Zeile, a slow runner, gave it all he could to score from first base. The Mets would add an insurance run on Bubba Trammell's sacrifice fly. Armando Benitez, who had blown a save opportunity in Game 1, came in to close the door on the Bronx Bombers.

Paul O'Neill hits an RBI triple in the fourth inning to give the Yankees the lead.

For a team that seemed on the brink of collapse, the Mets proved they were not dead yet. By impressively ending the mythical streaks of El Duque and the Yankees, the Mets seemed ready to start a streak of their own.

GAME 3: Mets 4, Yankees 2

N.Y. YANKEES	AB	R	H	BI	BB	SO	AVG
JVizcaino 2b	4	0	0	0	0	2	.286
Polonia ph	1	0	0	0	0	0	.500
Jeter ss	4	1	2	0	1	2	.462
Justice lf	3	0	1	1	1	0	.200
BeWilliams cf	4	0	0	0	0	2	.000
TMartinez 1b	3	1	1	0	1	1	.429
Posada c	4	0	0	0	0	2	.250
O'Neill rf	4	0	3	1	0	0	.583
Brosius 3b	2	0	0	0	0	1	.250
GHill ph	1	0	0	0	0	0	.000
Sojo 3b	0	0	0	0	0	0	.000
OHernandez p	2	0	0	0	0	2	.000
Stanton p	0	0	0	0	0	0	—
Knoblauch ph	1	0	1	0	0	0	.111
Totals	33	2	8	2	3	12	

N.Y. METS	AB	R	H	BI	BB	SO	AVG
Perez rf	3	0	0	0	1	1	.077
Alfonzo 2b	4	0	0	0	0	2	.154
Piazza c	4	1	1	0	0	2	.231
Ventura 3b	3	1	2	1	0	2	.250
Zeile 1b	4	1	2	1	0	2	.462
Agbayani lf	3	0	1	1	1	1	.364
McEwing pr-lf	0	1	0	0	0	0	.000
Payton cf	4	0	1	0	0	2	.231
Bordick ss	3	0	1	0	0	1	.167
LHarris ph	0	0	0	0	0	0	.000
Trammell ph	0	0	0	1	0	0	1.000
Benitez p	0	0	0	0	0	0	—
Reed p	1	0	1	0	0	0	1.000
Hamilton ph	1	0	0	0	0	0	.000
Wendell p	0	0	0	0	0	0	—
Cook p	0	0	0	0	0	0	—
JFranco p	0	0	0	0	0	0	—
KAbbott ph-ss	1	0	0	0	0	1	.250
Totals	31	4	9	4	3	13	

N.Y. YANKEES				001	100	000—2	8	0
N.Y. METS				010	001	02x—4	9	0

LOB—N.Y. Yankees 10, N.Y. Mets 8. **2B—**Justice (2), O'Neill (2), Piazza (1), Ventura (1), Zeile (2), Agbayani (2). **3B—**O'Neill (1). **HR—**Ventura (1) off OHernandez. **RBI—**Justice (3), O'Neill (2), Ventura (1), Zeile (1), Agbayani (1), Trammell (3). **S—**OHernandez, Reed. **SF—**Trammell. **DP—**N.Y. Mets 1

N.Y. YANKEES	IP	H	R	ER	BB	SO	NP	ERA
OHernandez L, 0-1	7⅓	9	4	4	3	12	134	4.91
Stanton	⅔	0	0	0	0	1	7	0.00

N.Y. METS	IP	H	R	ER	BB	SO	NP	ERA
Reed	6	6	2	2	1	8	102	3.00
Wendell	⅓	0	0	0	1	2	13	5.40
Cook	⅓	0	0	0	1	1	11	0.00
JFranco W, 1-0	1	1	0	0	0	0	9	0.00
Benitez S, 1	1	1	0	0	1	1	14	4.50

Cook pitched to 1 batter in 8th. **HBP—**by Cook (Justice), by Reed (Brosius). **Umpires—**Home, Kellogg; First, Welke, Tim; Second, McClelland; Third, Crawford; Left, Montague; Right, Reliford. **T—**3:39. **A—**55,299 (55,777).

Game 4

1-2-3 Victory

AP/WWP

Derek Jeter watches his first-pitch hit sail over the fence for a home run.

Wednesday, October 25, 2000, Shea Stadium. In life and in baseball, few things are as easy as 1-2-3. The Yankees were evidence of this, dropping a closely contested Game 3 that many had predicted them to win easily. For a team that had seen its advanced age at the center of attention, the Yankees proved they also possess the fountain of youth. Carried by the heroics of young superstar Derek Jeter, the Yankees showed that winning their 15th World Series game out of 16, while not easy, was a matter of 1-2-3.

1 – The number of pitches it took for the Yankees to take the lead and snatch the momentum away from the Mets.

AP/WWP

Bobby Jones was the Game 4 starter for the Mets.

2 – The uniform number of Yankees' shortstop Derek Jeter, who blasted the first-pitch, first-inning home run.

3 – The number of victories the Yankees would have at the end of the night to bring them one step away from their third consecutive world championship.

The Yankees Chip Away In Innings One, Two And Three

Only the 16th leadoff home run in World Series history, Jeter's blast off of Bobby Jones quieted the Shea Stadium crowd. After one inning, it was 1-0 Yankees. The defending champions were responding to their scrappy challengers in their trademark relentless style.

The critics had said they were too old. Too hurt. Too slow. But the Yankees, though they might be old-timers, proved to be spry old-timers when running the basepaths. In the second inning, 37-year-old outfielder Paul O'Neill legged out his second triple of the series. Scott Brosius' sacrifice fly scored O'Neill and after two, it was 2-0 Yankees.

AP/WWP

Paul O'Neill crosses the plate in the second inning.

In the third inning, Jeter again took center stage by belting a triple, later scoring on a ground out by Luis Sojo. Entering the bottom of the third, it was 3-0 Yankees. And that was all they would need.

The Mets Fight Back Valiantly

AP/WWP

Mike Piazza watches his two-run home run in the third inning.

The Mets shook the cobwebs off their bats in the bottom of the third. Mike Piazza, who seemed to have figured Yankees' starter Denny Neagle out with his monstrous foul in the first, erased any doubt that he had Neagle's number, hitting a two-run homer that reenergized the sagging spirits of the Shea Stadium faithful.

The Yankees bullpen of David Cone, Jeff Nelson and Mike Stanton held true and the score remained 3-2 going into the bottom of the eighth. Once again, the Yankees and Mets were in a nail-biter, but Mariano Rivera entered the game for the Yankees with one mission: to finish off the Mets. The seemingly invincible Rivera had given up two earned runs in the ninth inning of Game 2, but history would not repeat itself, as Rivera struck out two in two innings to earn his first save of the 2000 World Series. The title was within reach.

GAME 4: Yankees 3, Mets 2

N.Y. YANKEES	AB	R	H	BI	BB	SO	AVG
Jeter ss	5	2	2	1	0	1	.444
Sojo 2b	4	0	1	1	1	0	.167
Justice lf	5	0	0	0	0	0	.133
Bellinger lf	0	0	0	0	0	0	—
BeWilliams cf	4	0	0	0	0	1	.000
TMartinez 1b	4	0	2	0	0	1	.444
O'Neill rf	4	1	2	0	0	0	.563
Posada c	3	0	0	1	1	1	.200
Brosius 3b	1	0	1	1	2	0	.333
Neagle p	2	0	0	0	0	1	.000
Cone p	0	0	0	0	0	0	—
Canseco ph	1	0	0	0	0	1	.000
Nelson p	0	0	0	0	0	0	—
Stanton p	0	0	0	0	0	0	—
MRivera p	1	0	0	0	0	0	.000
Totals	34	3	8	3	4	6	

N.Y. METS	AB	R	H	BI	BB	SO	AVG
Perez rf	3	1	1	0	0	1	.125
KAbbott ph-ss	1	0	0	0	0	1	.200
Alfonzo 2b	3	0	0	0	1	0	.125
Piazza c	4	1	1	2	0	1	.235
Zeile 1b	4	0	2	0	0	0	.471
McEwing pr	0	0	0	0	0	0	.000
Benitez p	0	0	0	0	0	0	—
Ventura 3b	4	0	0	0	0	0	.188
Agbayani lf	3	0	0	1	1	1	.286
Payton cf	4	0	2	0	0	1	.294
Bordick ss	2	0	0	0	0	0	.125
LHarris ph	0	0	0	0	1	0	.000
JFranco p	0	0	0	0	0	0	—
MFranco 1b	1	0	0	0	0	1	.000
BJJones p	2	0	0	0	0	1	.000
Rusch p	0	0	0	0	0	0	—
Hamilton ph	0	0	0	0	0	0	.000
Trammell ph-rf	1	0	0	0	0	1	.500
Totals	32	2	6	2	3	8	

N.Y. YANKEES	111	000	000—3	8 0
N.Y. METS	002	000	000—2	6 1

E—Trammell (1). LOB—N.Y. Yankees 9, N.Y. Mets 6. 3B—Jeter (1), O'Neill (2). HR—Piazza (2) off Neagle; Jeter (1) off BJJones. RBI—Jeter (1), Sojo (1), Brosius (3), Piazza 2 (4). SB—Sojo (1). SF—Brosius. DP—N.Y. Yankees 1; N.Y. Mets 1.

N.Y. YANKEES	IP	H	R	ER	BB	SO	NP	ERA
Neagle	4⅔	4	2	2	3	3	73	3.86
Cone	⅓	0	0	0	0	0	5	0.00
Nelson W, 1-0	1⅓	1	0	0	1	1	23	10.13
Stanton	⅔	0	0	0	0	2	7	0.00
MRivera S, 1	2	1	0	0	0	2	28	3.60

N.Y. METS	IP	H	R	ER	BB	SO	NP	ERA
BJJones L, 0-1	5	4	3	3	3	3	74	5.40
Rusch	2	3	0	0	0	2	37	2.25
JFranco	1	1	0	0	0	1	8	0.00
Benitez	1	0	0	0	1	0	23	3.00

Umpires—Home, Welke, Tim; First, McCleiland; Second, Crawford; Third, Montague; Left, Reliford; Right, Kellogg. T—3:20. A—55,290 (55,777).

Game 5
So-jo Dramatic

The Yankees celebrate their Subway Series championship.

Thursday, October 26, 2000, Shea Stadium. The fifth game of the Subway Series was a must-win for the Mets. They had to ensure that their final home game of the season wouldn't be their final game of the season.

Would Mets' starting pitcher Al Leiter be able to earn his first post-season win? He had 11 postseason starts under his belt and no wins to show for it. Surely, the Mets fans felt, his time had come. After all, other postseason consecutive streaks had fallen during this series. Orlando Hernandez finally lost a postseason game after earning eight straight victories without a loss. With Hernandez's loss, the Yankees lost another streak, too: their first World Series game in 15 competitions. Yes, the fans thought, Leiter will light the fire and lead the Mets to victory.

The pitching matchup in this game was the same as in Game 1: Leiter against Yankees left-hander Andy Pettitte. Mets manager Bobby Valentine shook up his lineup in an attempt to generate some offense. Rookie sensation Timo Perez was benched in favor of reserve outfielder Bubba Trammell. Perez was red-hot in the two previous series, but couldn't get anything going against the Yankees. Shortstop Mike Bordick was out too, in favor of Kurt Abbott. The Yankees kept their

AP/WWP

lineup largely the same. Luis Sojo had started second base in Game 4, but manager Joe Torre went with Jose Vizcaino, who had great success against Leiter in Game 1.

Al Leiter looked to carry the Mets on his shoulders in Game 5.

The first inning was uneventful. When Bernie Williams came up to bat at the top of the second inning, he seemed an unlikely threat. The Yankees' star center fielder, who was the team's leading RBI man in the regular season, couldn't buy a hit in the Subway Series, going 0-for-15 in the first four games. But Williams smacked a Leiter pitch over the left-field wall for his first hit and first home run of the 2000 World Series. He had broken his run of bad luck.

The Mets came right back in the bottom of the inning and it was Leiter who led the way. With two out and runners on second and third, the gutsy pitcher laid down a bunt. First baseman Tino Martinez ran in to get the ball and tossed to Pettitte covering

AP/WWP

Bernie Williams smacks a home run in the second inning.

first. Pettitte bobbled the ball, allowing Trammell to score and moving Jay Payton to third base. Benny Agbayani followed with a slow roller to third that took a wicked hop on Scott Brosius. He couldn't make the

Benny Agbayani hits a slow roller that scores a run.

play and Payton ran home. Pettitte got out of the inning having given up two unearned runs.

Mets fans had some hope. Maybe, just maybe, the Mets could battle their way to victory and force a Game 6 at Yankee Stadium.

The Yankees tied things up in the sixth when Derek Jeter hit a solo home run to left that looked eerily similar to Williams' blast in the second. It was Jeter's 14th consecutive World Series game with a hit.

It Looks Like Another Long One

In the eighth inning Pettitte was done, but Leiter was still going strong. This game was *his* game and he was not going to surrender. By the time the game reached the ninth inning, Leiter had thrown more than 120 pitches, but he still had his stuff, striking out Martinez and

O'Neill. It looked like this game might go into extra innings, just like Game 1 had. But then Jorge Posada came up to bat and worked a walk off of Leiter. Yet Leiter stayed in the game. Brosius came up and smacked a single into left field, advancing Posada to second. Still, Leiter stayed in. You could tell by looking into the eyes of the fierce competitor that, despite his tiring arm, Leiter would not let his team down.

Derek Jeter shows his home run stroke in the sixth inning.

The light-hitting Luis Sojo, who came into the game in the eighth inning when Vizcaino was lifted for a pinch hitter, came up to bat. Leiter hurled his 142nd pitch of the game toward the plate. Sojo whacked it into center field past the diving middle infielders for a single. Posada rushed home from second base as the throw from center fielder Jay Payton came toward catcher Mike Piazza. But Payton's throw never reached Piazza – it hit Posada and skittered into the Mets' dugout. Posada scored and

APWWP

Jorge Posada scores the winning run.

Brosius followed right after him, giving the Yankees the lead, 4-2.

Sojo's hit finally chased Leiter, the tragic hero. After veteran John Franco came in and retired pinch hitter Glenallen Hill, the Mets were down to their final three outs.

The Yankees put their ace reliever Mariano Rivera in to pitch the bottom half of the ninth inning. Rivera struck out Darryl Hamilton, walked Benny Agbayani, then got his second out from Edgardo Alfonzo. If anyone could turn the game around with one swing, it would be Mike Piazza, who now stepped to the plate. The hearts of Mets fans skipped a beat as Piazza lifted a towering fly to center field. But Bernie Williams drifted under it and snared the ball for the final out. After making the catch, Williams bent down on one knee as if in prayer, and then jumped up to join his teammates celebrating their World Series victory on the pitcher's mound.

GAME 5: Yankees 4, Mets 2

N.Y. YANKEES	AB	R	H	BI	BB	SO	AVG
JVizcaino 2b	3	0	0	0	0	1	.235
Knoblauch ph	1	0	0	0	0	0	.100
Stanton p	0	0	0	0	0	0	—
GHill ph	1	0	0	0	0	0	.000
MRivera p	0	0	0	0	0	0	.000
Jeter ss	4	1	1	1	1	0	2	.409
Justice lf	4	0	1	0	0	1	.158
Bellinger lf	0	0	0	0	0	0	—
BeWilliams cf	3	1	2	1	1	1	.111
TMartinez 1b	4	0	0	0	0	1	.364
O'Neill rf	3	0	0	0	1	2	.474
Posada c	3	1	1	0	1	0	.222
Brosius 3b	4	1	1	0	0	0	.308
Pettitte p	3	0	0	0	0	1	.000
Sojo 2b	1	0	1	1	0	0	.286
Totals	34	4	7	3	3	9	

N.Y. METS	AB	R	H	BI	BB	SO	AVG
Agbayani lf	4	0	1	1	1	1	.278
Alfonzo 2b	5	0	1	0	0	0	.143
Piazza c	5	0	2	0	0	0	.273
Zeile 1b	3	0	0	0	1	2	.400
Ventura 3b	4	0	0	0	0	2	.150
Trammell rf	3	1	1	0	1	0	.400
Perez rf	0	0	0	0	0	0	.125
Payton cf	4	1	2	0	0	1	.333
KAbbott ss	3	0	1	0	1	0	.250
ALeiter p	2	0	0	0	0	0	.000
JFranco p	0	0	0	0	0	0	—
Hamilton ph	1	0	0	0	0	1	.000
Totals	34	2	8	1	4	7	

N.Y. YANKEES	010 001 002—4	7	1
N.Y. METS	020 000 000—2	8	1

E—Pettitte (1), Payton (2). LOB—N.Y. Yankees 6, N.Y. Mets 10. 2B—Piazza (2). HR—Jeter (2) off ALeiter; BeWilliams (1) off ALeiter. RBI—Jeter (2), BeWilliams (1), Sojo (2), Agbayani (2). S—ALeiter.

N.Y. YANKEES	IP	H	R	ER	BB	SO	NP	ERA
Pettitte	7	8	2	0	3	5	125	1.98
Stanton W, 2-0	1	0	0	0	0	1	14	0.00
MRivera S, 2	1	0	0	0	1	1	13	3.00

N.Y. METS	IP	H	R	ER	BB	SO	NP	ERA
ALeiter L, 0-1	8⅔	7	4	3	3	9	142	2.87
JFranco	⅓	0	0	0	0	0	6	0.00

Umpires—Home, McClelland; First, Crawford; Second, Montague; Third, Reliford; Left, Kellogg; Right, Welke, Tim. T—3:32. A—55,292 (55,777).

Subway Series 2000: A Look Back

The 14th Subway Series ended just after midnight on Friday, October 27, 2000. The Yankees came away victorious yet again, capturing their 26th world championship in the process. It was also the Yankees' 11th Subway Series championship, and their first-ever World Series win over the crosstown New York Mets.

Tino Martinez, Chuck Knoblauch and Jose Vizcaino celebrate the Yankees' 26th World Series championship.

As Bernie Williams pulled down Mike Piazza's fly ball for the final out, the Yankees rushed to the pitcher's mound to celebrate their victory. Arms in the air, whooping with joy, the players, coaches and manager hugged each other, shook hands and exchanged slaps on the back.

Bernie Williams and Roger Clemens carry manager Joe Torre on their shoulders.

As the team headed back into the clubhouse for the presentation of the World Series trophy and Most Valuable Player award, the Yankees hoisted manager Joe Torre up on their shoulders in triumph. Torre, overcome, broke down in tears. This championship-thing just never gets old.

The tears continued in the clubhouse when Yankees' owner George Steinbrenner was presented with the championship trophy. Steinbrenner, known more for ruling with an iron fist than for being the warm-and-fuzzy type, thanked his team and manager for their accomplishments and congratulated the Mets for their worthy opposition. Derek

MVP Derek Jeter's 2000 World Series Stats	
Games Played:	5
At Bats:	22
Hits:	9
Batting Average:	.407
Runs Scored:	6
Doubles:	2
Triples:	1
Home Runs:	2
RBI:	2
Walks:	3

AP/WWP

Derek Jeter's solo home run in the sixth inning of Game 5 helped him earn World Series MVP honors.

Jeter, a Yankees leader on and off the playing field, was named the series' Most Valuable Player.

Although the Mets pulled out only one victory in five chances, they were formidable competitors for the Yankees. Three of the five games were decided by one run and the other two were decided by two runs. Jeter called the Mets "the best team we've played in my years here." That was quite a compliment considering that in Jeter's five years with the Yankees, he's faced three other World Series opponents, including the mighty Atlanta Braves twice.

The difference between the two teams boiled down to pitching. The Yankees' batters worked 25 walks off the Mets' mound, while the Mets were free swingers and received a paltry 11 free bases. The Mets' impatient bats allowed the pinstriped pitchers to record 48 strikeouts while the Mets racked up 40.

Game-By-Game Recap		
GAME	SCORE	WINNER
1	4-3	Yankees
2	6-5	Yankees
3	4-2	Mets
4	3-2	Yankees
5	4-2	Yankees

AP/WWP

A couple of World Series records were broken during the Subway Series. Game 1 went into the record books as the longest game (by time) in World Series history, taking 4 hours, 51 minutes to determine a winner, and the Yankees beat their own record of 12 consecutive World Series wins by winning 14 games in a row. Congratulations to the world champion New York Yankees!

Yankees' owner George Steinbrenner and Joe Torre rejoice in receiving the 2000 World Series Championship trophy.

The Victory Parade

The parade route is deluged with confetti as the Yankees' championship is celebrated.

The victory parade down New York City's Canyon of Heroes took place Monday, October 30, just after noon, giving the Bronx Bombers three days to recover from their grueling season and subsequent victory celebrations.

It was a chilly day in the Big Apple, but millions of die-hard Yankee fans braved the cold and played hooky from school and work to show their team their appreciation and admiration. Paper and confetti rained from the sky even before the parade celebrating the Yankees' championship reign officially began.

Led by Grand Marshal Yogi Berra, the triumphant Yankees traveled the parade route in lower Manhattan for the fourth time in five years. The Yankee players seemed just as excited as fans were, using their position from atop the floats to videotape and photograph the momentous parade. Infielders Derek Jeter, Chuck Knoblauch, Tino Martinez and Scott Brosius waved to the crowd as they stood atop a float that proudly proclaimed "Derek Jeter MVP."

The World Series Championship trophy accompanied the float that included Yankee manager Joe Torre, his coaching staff and New York City mayor Rudy Giuliani, among others.

Giuliani, an avowed Yankees fan, had offered the

Yogi Berra led the parade and served as Grand Marshal.

27

New York Mets an opportunity to participate in the parade as well, but the Mets declined.

AP/WWP

Tino Martinez (top left), Derek Jeter (top right with video camera) and friends take in the parade.

"It was a generous offer on behalf of the mayor," Mets' general manager Steve Phillips remarked. But, he continued, "It should be the Yankees' day. They deserve the stage to themselves." Several Mets' players agreed, including outfielder Darryl Hamilton. "When you win you should have all the glory."

The Mets will get their day in the sun when they are recognized in a ceremony at City Hall at a later date.

For the Yankees, their ceremony at City Hall began with each player receiving a key to the city. The mayor gave team owner George Steinbrenner the first key, followed by team management, the coaches and the players.

Stepping to the podium, Torre had nothing but words of admiration for his players, saying, "They may get tired, but they never get tired of winning." He then turned the podium over to Andy Pettitte, who admitted, "It's a really special team we have."

Although not all of the players honored in the ceremony will be back in pinstripes in 2001, the 2000 Yankees will forever be remembered for their pride, their power and their extraordinary perseverance.

AP/WWP

The World Series trophy took center stage on Yankee manager Joe Torre's float.

New York State Of Mind
– Why We Love The Yankees And The Mets

For the first time in 44 years, two New York teams would play against each other in the World Series, and New York became a city torn in two. And as you know, when you're a die-hard Yankees or Mets fan, the passion seeps into your blood (and sometimes goes to your head!). Here's a look at some of the teams' great fans from all across the country.

Marty Goldstein – Bobby V. Was Watching Me

On a trip to San Diego for some rest and relaxation, my wife and I decided to attend a Padres game. Our favorite baseball team, the Mets, were in town, and needed our support. Before the game, a Padres public relations agent spotted my golf jersey and asked if I would like to participate in the "Callaway Closest To The Pin Contest" right before game time. After manually closing my jaw, I agreed, and soon found myself in back of third base in front of the Mets dugout, with a pitching wedge in my hand. Bobby Valentine and the Mets were watching me this time, instead of the other way around.

I was pitted against another fan and got to within 15 feet on my first try. My shot netted me a Callaway Big Bertha Driver, prime time on stadium vision (with a re-run in the 5th inning) and an opportunity to shake hands with Bobby while he read a newspaper in the dugout. My wife even had me take a picture of her and Rey Ordonez. The glow of that experience still burns to this day. What luck . . . a couple of bumpkins from Connecticut stumble into Mets nirvana — it was like winning the lottery.

Marty Goldstein of Cheshire, Connecticut.

Jessica & Tim Turner – A House Divided

She says: I had to go and marry a Mets fan. I was secretly hoping this day wouldn't arrive for a few more years. I thought we could avoid this moment until our son could at least hold a bat in his pudgy, dimpled hands. But now, at four months old, Seamus' baseball fidelity hangs in the balance – as does the quality of a previously joyous marriage. I've been a die-hard Yankee fan my entire life. I always assumed my kids would be Yankee fans, too, but alas, Seamus' father has drawn

It's not too early to try to sway young Seamus' loyalty in the Turner household in Cambridge, Massachusetts.

a line in the sand. When the Yankees clinched the American League pennant, I barely showed any emotion for fear of the wrath of the storming Met fan – otherwise known as my husband Tim. The day after Seamus was born his proud new grandfather whipped a Derek Jeter T-shirt out of a plastic bag; I'll sneak it on Seamus when Daddy isn't watching.

He says: Enough about the Yankees. I've been waiting 14 years for the Mets to make it back to the World Series. Sure, 14 years isn't that long to wait, especially considering what Red Sox fans have gone through for the last century. But now the Mets are back and I'm in all my glory. My fanaticism was born out of the '86 season when the Mets won 108 games and the World Series in such dramatic fashion that you still find it replayed on the ESPN Classic sports network. Lenny Dykstra, Keith Hernandez, Gary Carter – those were great games. Now I feel reborn that the Mets have made it back to the World Series, but I have to share it with my wife – the Yankee fan. I guess this will be a lesson in consideration; however, if it gets too intense I may let out a few expletives and go walk the dog. As far as our infant son's allegiance is concerned, well, I don't think he'll remember these games. But if it takes constant reinforcement and exposure to a team to grow up a fan, then I think Daddy will win in the end. Let's go Mets!

Melissa Miller – The Yankees Will Always Have A Place In My Heart

When I was 7 years old, my father introduced me to what has become one of my greatest passions. It happened one night in our living room as I watched a group of men on television hitting a ball with a bat. These were the Yankees, my dad explained, and they were the greatest baseball team of all time. Father always knows best. From that day forward, I was hooked. I was the "son" my father never had, and watching baseball led to playing it. For several years I was the only girl on my team. Dad was there to watch my games and cheer me on. And we spent many a night in front of the TV, watching Bucky Dent and Willie Randolph turn a double play.

Melissa Miller of Plainville, Connecticut with some of her Yankees memorabilia.

I cried myself to sleep when Yankee captain and catcher Thurman Munson was killed in a 1979 plane crash. And when Bucky Dent was traded in the early 1980s, I vowed to boycott the team I loved. A few years went by, and I began to miss them. When I finally tuned them in again, I was instantly taken with a young first baseman named Don Mattingly. A gentleman both on and off the field, Mattingly played with such intensity that it was hard not to respect him. He became my new hero, and my love for the Yankees deepened. I watched Mattingly in pinstripes for more than a decade, but, sadly, after the 1995 season he was forced to retire due to nagging back injuries. He never saw a World Series. These days, I have no real favorite. I don't know that I will ever be taken with a player again the way I was with Donnie Baseball. The Yankees were the team of the last century and they will continue to dominate in this century. They will always have a special place in my heart.

Kevin DiStasio – I Snuck Into The World Series

I've been a Yankees fan since I can remember. My greatest triumph was sneaking into Game 1 of the 1998 World Series at Yankee Stadium. Yankee Stadium is like a fortress, so doing this required some ingenuity, and some good ol' fashioned running!

I hadn't been to Yankee Stadium in a long time, so I wanted to be around the Stadium for Game 1. Paying a ticket scalper $500 was not going to happen, so we devised a plan to get in. My friend Mark noticed an unattended handicapped access gate (Jesus, please forgive me). The gate was right next to the turnstiles at the entry gate. I opened

Kevin DiStasio of Atlanta, Georgia.

the gate just enough to sneak in and proceeded to calmly walk inside the Stadium. I didn't even look back to see if Mark and my brother David (who had joined us in our scheme) were behind me.

Just as I was about to blend in with the crowd, a voice bellowed, "Where's your tickets?!" I turned around while patting my pockets, as if searching for the tickets, and noticed then that Mark and David were behind me. They followed my cue, and began looking for tickets. The security guy was standing next to us by now, while the three of us played the game of "Uh, do you have the tickets? I thought you had them?" When the guard turned his head to see if anyone else was coming in, we all bolted through the tunnels of Yankee Stadium! Unfortunately for us, we all took off in separate directions and weren't able to find each other during the game, but the good news was that the guard was unable to get any of us. I sat in an unoccupied seat in the upper deck, right behind home plate, and watched the Yanks come from behind on Tino Martinez's grand slam homer to take Game 1 of the World Series from the Padres. And I did it all for free!

Mike LoDico – Heaven Has A New Center Fielder

Sometimes our heroes are our father's heroes. My father's hero was Joseph Paul DiMaggio. Both were born in 1914. My father was an Italian-American and Sicilian. He grew up in the 1930s when there was still prejudice against anyone whose last name ended in a vowel. While many people still struggled to pronounce the name DiMaggio in

Mike LoDico of Boulder Creek, California.

1939, my father and his friends had found their first role model. I never saw DiMaggio play baseball because I was born in 1951, a few months after his retirement from the Yankees.

At family gatherings, when the topic turned to baseball, my father would open his wallet and take out the picture of his hero – Joe DiMaggio. The 56-game hitting streak, big hits to beat the hated Red Sox, playoff games, home runs and clutch catches were all detailed by my dad to anyone who would listen. My dad could easily recall all of DiMaggio's stats.

Watching the news clips and television specials in black and white, the fluid grace and quiet, gentle presence of the man were easy to see. I made Joe DiMaggio my hero and role model. My father passed on in 1969 when I was 16. He never met his hero in person. When I moved to the San Francisco Bay area I visited Joe DiMaggio's restaurant and I wished my dad could have been there with me at the bar for a drink and a story. I touched Joe DiMaggio's sleeve at the Oakland Coliseum. I saw DiMaggio on the news in San Francisco just after the 1989 earthquake. I thought of what my dad would think and what he would have been like at age 75. Today I know two things: Heaven's team has a new center fielder and my dad has finally met his hero.

Eric Fedor – I Think About The Mets All Day Long

I am 10 years old and I am a die-hard Mets fan. I love the Mets. I've been a fan my whole life, but started following them closely only a couple of years ago. Since I live in New York, I have a choice of two baseball teams to root for. The Mets are the team I've chosen, mostly because of their dramatic games. I never lose faith in the Amazin's. They can always stage a comeback.

My favorite player is second baseman Edgardo Alfonzo. He has a great ability to get a big hit when the game is on the line, and he is in

Eric Fedor of New York.

every dramatic inning the Mets have. His offense isn't his only incredible talent. He can also make any defensive play he needs to make.

I go to many games each year. The Mets can always make some magic when I'm there. I once saw them come back from a four-run deficit in the ninth inning versus the Phillies. I'm very loud when I root for the Mets, whether at Shea or at home. This year the Mets have done many great things. When I see a great thing happen I feel not just excited, but also happy. This is because I think about the Mets all day long. So when something good and exciting happens, I get to think good thoughts. Even when the Mets are not doing well, I still think about them, and I always try to think good things about the Mets.

This year the Mets made it to the World Series. This series is historic because for the first time in 44 years, two New York teams are in the World Series, which now is being called the Subway Series. This makes the usually exciting World Series even more exciting. Whoever wins will get the unofficial title of being the top team of the Big Apple and their fans will get bragging rights. No matter who you're rooting for, or who wins, the series will be very fun and exciting.

Bradford H. Turnow – Yankee Fever Has Caught Me

My love of the New York Yankees began when I was growing up in New York in the late 1970s. The excitement of the 1977 and 1978 World Series games hooked me forever. Yankee fever caught me and hasn't let go ever since.

I am a New York Yankees fanatic. I live and breathe the Yankees. I have collected Yankee memorabilia for almost 20 years. I own many great items, but there are two that stand out and mean more to me than any others. The first is a large poster-sized lithograph depicting "The Mighty Mick of '56" and it is autographed by Mickey Mantle. My

Bradford H. Turnow (left) of Hampton Bays, New York with Yankee skipper Joe Torre (right).

favorite piece is a 20" x 24" picture autographed by almost the entire 1996 championship team, which shows them cheering after the final out of that championship game.

A lot of fans jumped off the bandwagon in the 1980s because of our departure from postseason thrills, but I hung on and cheered for my Yankees. My two favorite Yankees of all-time are Mantle and Ruth. Mickey Charles Mantle was the glory and pride of a Yankees team that dominated the era like no other, and George Herman "Babe" Ruth was simply the greatest athlete to play any sport at any time in history.

I have many great Yankee memories, but I have one that will stay with me forever – meeting the Yankee skipper, Joe Torre. I met him at a book signing on Long Island. It was about a two-hour wait, but boy, was it worth it. Even having already signed many, many books, he greeted every person like he or she was the first. When he agreed to pose for a photo, I knew I had a memory I could share for generations to come. I have been lucky to meet many athletes in my time, but none will ever compare to the encounter I had with Joe Torre.

Bob Saunders – How Can The Mets Be In Southern California Without Me?

I've been a Mets fan since 1963 when my father took me to the Polo Grounds to see the Mets play. The Mets were awful back then, and my father used to laugh at how bad they were. At that game, Jimmy Piersall hit his 100th career home run and ran around the bases backwards (right order – just backwards) and the fans were going nuts! I fell in love and have been a Mets fan ever since.

Bob Saunders of Los Angeles.

As a kid growing up on Long Island, I idolized the Mets. Ron Swoboda was one of my heroes. His nickname was "Rocky," and he was the first young Met to display any hitting power. I would go to the games at Shea and scream myself hoarse.

I've lived in Los Angeles since 1976 and haven't missed a visit by the Mets to LA since 1977 or to the ballpark in San Diego since about 1984. How can the Mets be in Southern California without me? In 1988, I went to every playoff game for the National League pennant between the Dodgers and Mets. We lost   in the seventh game at Dodger Stadium and I was heartbroken as all those happy Dodger fans surrounded me, screaming "Beat New York."

My favorite moment (up till now) was in the 1986 World Series, when Mookie Wilson (my favorite Met ever) hit a ground ball that got through Bill Buckner's legs. The sheer joy from winning that Series was overwhelming. In 1997, I went to a game at Shea for the first time in about 24 years. It was a nice day and I took the #7 train from the city to Shea. I was happy to be back in my old stomping grounds, but as I got off the train and walked to take a photo of the stadium, the sky opened up – rain, thunder, hail and lightning – the works. I thought to myself – that's a fine how-do-you-do! Despite several rain delays, the Mets won. Now there's finally a World Series against the Yanks. Amazing. LET'S GO METS!

Big Apple Battles
– Past Subway Series Matchups

New York Yankees vs. Brooklyn Dodgers

Between 1923 and 1939, the Yankees won eight world championships (including four straight from 1936 and 1939) and were the toast of the greatest city in the world. With the Giants' days as a powerhouse finished, the Yankees were *the* team in New York, with future Hall-of-Famers Joe DiMaggio, Bill Dickey and Lou Gehrig.

For loyal Brooklyn Dodgers fans, this just gave them one more team to hate! The lovable losers from Brooklyn (nicknamed "The Boys of Summer") hadn't won a pennant since 1920 and always played an "also-ran" to the Giants in the National League. But that changed in 1941, when the Dodgers finally rewarded their long-suffering fans with a pennant under the watch of manager Leo Durocher. Now the Dodgers set to do battle with the powerful American League champion Yankees in their first Subway Series.

The ball gets past Brooklyn Dodgers catcher Mickey Owen in a dramatic moment of the 1941 World Series.

The 1941 battle between New York and Brooklyn was seen as a battle of the "haves" and the "never-coulds," of the "suits" and the "overalls." Although all the games were close, it was the fateful Game 4 that convinced many that the Yankees were blessed and the Dodgers were cursed!

The first two games in Yankee Stadium were decided by one run, with the Yankees taking Game 1 by a 3-2 score and the Dodgers scratching out a 3-2 win in Game 2. The next game was scoreless in the seventh inning until Brooklyn pitcher Freddie Fitzsimmons was hit on the knee by a line drive and couldn't continue. The Yankees then knocked around the reliever Hugh Casey to win the game.

That freak play involving Fitzsimmons was just an omen of worse things to come for Brooklyn. Leading 4-3 in the 9th inning of an

important Game 4, the Dodgers had Casey on the mound again. After two groundouts, it was up to Yankees right-fielder, "Ol' Reliable" Tommy Henrich. On a two-strike pitch, Casey threw a breaking ball in the dirt (many believe it was a spitball) and Heinrich swung and missed for strike three. But catcher Mickey Owen let the pitch skip past him and Heinrich was safe on first.

Yankee great Joe DiMaggio greets Tommy Henrich at the plate after Henrich clouts a home run in Game 5 of the 1941 World Series.

The Yankees made good use of their new life, pounding out four runs with two out and beating Brooklyn 7-4 in front of 34,000 devastated fans at Ebbets Field. The Yankees then beat their downtrodden foes at Ebbets again in Game 5 to take the series.

The Yankees and Dodgers would not meet again until 1947, the year Brooklyn infielder Jackie Robinson broke baseball's color barrier. The 1947 series was the first to be broadcast on television, and baseball fans couldn't ask for a better matchup than the archrival Yankees and Dodgers.

In a sloppily pitched series that set a record for walks and wild pitches, the Yankees took the first two games at home, including a 10-3 slaughter in Game 2. Brooklyn outslugged their rivals 9-8 in Game 3, surviving the first-ever World Series pinch-hit homer (by Yankee catcher Yogi Berra).

But with all that poor pitching, would you believe Game 4 nearly put

Jackie Robinson of the Dodgers in 1947.

the first World Series no-hitter into the record books? Yankees pitcher Bill Bevens posted a 7-13 record that year, but it didn't mean a thing when he held the Dodgers hitless for 8-2/3 innings (although he walked a staggering 10 batters). Then, with runners on first and second and the

Yankees up 2-1, Brooklyn's Cookie Lavagetto laced a pinch-hit double to right center that not only broke up the no-hitter, but won the game! The ecstatic Brooklyn fans stormed the field as their heroes high-tailed it to the dugout with their stolen Game 4 victory.

Jackie Robinson steals home in the 1955 World Series against the Yankees.

The Yankees bounced back to win Game 5, setting up a crucial Game 6 and another classic World Series moment, this time before 74,000 screaming fans in Yankee Stadium. With Brooklyn up 8-5 in the sixth, the Yankees had two men on and two out. Joe DiMaggio, who already had two homers in the series, belted a 415-foot drive to the bullpen in left center. Dodgers left fielder Al Gionfriddo (inserted as a defensive replacement) sprinted all the way from the left field line and made a sensational catch that robbed DiMaggio of a home run and saved the game for Brooklyn. But in the end, the mighty Yankees took the series, turning back the upstart challengers in a 5-2 win before a joyous Yankee Stadium crowd.

Joe DiMaggio takes a swing late in the 1949 regular season.

Two years later, the two teams hooked up again in their third battle for Big Apple bragging rights. Both the Yankees and the Dodgers snuck into the World Series by one game in 1949. The exciting regular-season finish carried over into the World Series, as Brooklyn and New York scratched and clawed through a series whose five games were decided by only eight runs. After the Yankees' Allie Reynolds and the Dodgers' Preacher Roe traded tense 1-0 wins in

Games 1 and 2, the Yankees took Games 3 and 4 and shut the door on the series by pummeling Brooklyn 10-6 in Game 5. Despite hitting .226 for the series, the Yankees asserted their dominance yet again.

New faces were a big story in this series, including first-year Yankee manager and former Brooklyn skipper Casey Stengel, Dodgers catcher Roy Campanella and rookie pitcher Don Newcombe.

The 1949 series was the beginning of a streak of five straight Yankees champion-ships and in 1952, they

Left to right, Yankees Jackie Jensen, Joe DiMaggio and Billy Martin at spring training in 1950.

were poised to win another on the backs of veterans Berra and Rizzuto and youngsters Mickey Mantle and Billy Martin. But Brooklyn had a great team too, with a core of Robinson, Campanella, Duke Snider, Gil Hodges and pitcher Carl Erskine.

The Dodgers went up 3-2 in the series, thanks mostly to timely hitting by Snider and an 11-inning complete game by Erskine in Game 5. But the Yankees struck back with a 3-2 win in Game 6 that featured late-inning homers by Berra and Mantle and a ground ball single off the knee of Brooklyn pitcher Billy Loes, who claimed he lost it in the sun!

Game 7 brought another dramatic World Series moment, and another championship to the Yankees. With the Yanks up 4-2 in the seventh, Brooklyn loaded the bases with two out. Jackie Robinson hit a little pop fly to the right of the mound, but inexplica-bly, no one moved to catch it! As the Brooklyn runners raced around the bases, rookie second baseman Billy Martin dashed in and made a

Jackie Robinson of the Dodgers places a bunt down the first base line in the 1949 World Series.

fantastic knee-high catch to preserve the lead and win the series. Once again, the Yankees proved that no matter how good the competition was, they were better!

The Brooklyn Dodgers celebrate a Game 3 victory in the 1953 World Series. Brooklyn's Don Zimmer wears #9.

If the Dodger faithful were frustrated at yet another World Series loss to the Yankees, they had to be buoyed by Brooklyn's 105 regular-season wins in 1953. Some have called the 1953 Dodgers one of the greatest teams ever, as Snider and Campanella each hit over 40 home runs, Carl Furillo led the league with a .344 average, and Erskine racked up 20 wins.

But Casey Stengel's Yankees ran over the American League again and geared up for another World Series. Brooklyn's hitters had the bigger stats, but the Yankees had great team players like Martin, Rizzuto, McDougald, Mantle and Berra. New York's pitching staff, anchored by Whitey Ford, Eddie Lopat and Allie Reynolds, had an amazing ERA of 2.43.

But hitting would dominate the series, specifically the hot bat of Billy Martin. The series featured great individual feats, such as Carl Erskine's 14 strikeouts in Game 3 and Mickey Mantle's grand slam in Game 5, but it was the feisty Martin who almost single-handedly powered the Yankees to victory in six games. Among his 12 series hits were a bases-loaded triple in Game 1,

Mickey Mantle bashes a grand slam off of Russ Meyer in Game 5 of the 1953 World Series.

home runs in Games 2 and 5, and a game-winning single in Game 6 – with each game a New York victory. The Yankees' victory train rolled on while miserable Dodger fans could only shout "Wait 'til next year!"

When "next year" finally came, the two teams found themselves nose-to-nose again in the 1955 World Series. Stengel's Yankees won

96 games, had a superstar in Mantle and boasted great pitching. Brooklyn also had a great staff and the usual suspects – Robinson, Snider, Campanella, Hodges, Reese – were back and ready to battle the Yankees.

But would the outcome be different this year? It didn't look that way at first, as the Yankees won Games 1 and 2 with a great combi-

A pair of all-time great catchers, Roy Campanella of the Dodgers and Yogi Berra of the Yankees.

nation of timely hitting and gritty pitching. Even Jackie Robinson's amazing steal of home in Game 1 couldn't help Brooklyn's cause.

But Johnny Podres stopped the Yankees cold in Game 3, anchoring an 8-3 Brooklyn win on his 23rd birthday. The Dodgers slugged three homers to take Game 4 and Snider hit two homers to help take Game 5 for Brooklyn. The Dodgers were on the cusp of that elusive championship but the gusty Yankees won Game 6 on Whitey Ford's four-hitter and Brooklyn fans feared the other shoe would drop in Game 7.

With Game 3 hero Podres protecting a 2-0 lead for Brooklyn, Yogi Berra came up in the bottom of the sixth with two on and one out. Berra sliced a drive toward the left field corner that spelled doom for Brooklyn, but left fielder

Dodgers hurler Johnny Podres, shown here in 1955.

Sandy Amoros raced all the way over from left center and made a spectacular catch. He then threw the ball to Reese who threw to first to complete a double play and preserved the lead for the Dodgers. The Yankees had another chance in the 8th, but Hank Bauer struck out with the tying runs on base.

And then the unbelievable happened. The Yankees went down 1-2-3 in the ninth, and before a Yankee Stadium crowd 63,000-strong, the Dodgers celebrated their first championship!

But the Yankees would get the last word on their 16-year long subway rivalry with the Dodgers when the two teams squared off for the

AP/WWP

final time in 1956. The matchup would not only result in another Yankees championship, but also feature one of the greatest pitching performance in World Series history.

The Dodgers seemed well on their way to a second championship after taking Games 1 and 2 behind the hot bat of Gil Hodges. But the

Don Larsen throws a perfect game in 1956.

Yankees roared back, with Ford and Tom Sturdivant throwing complete-game victories in Games 3 and 4.

But these great performances paled next to Yankee pitcher Don Larsen's feat in Game 5. Early in the game, neither Larsen nor Brooklyn's Sal "the Barber" Maglie had allowed a base runner. Mantle took care of Maglie's perfect game with a homer in the fourth, but Larsen kept throwing strikes and getting Dodger hitters out. The only close calls were balls hit by Jackie Robinson (a liner off the third baseman that caromed to the shortstop, who threw Robinson out) and Hodges (a drive to center backhanded by Mantle).

After 8-2/3 innings of three-up and three-down, Larsen struck out Dale Mitchell to put his perfect game in the record books. The Yankee Stadium crowd went bananas, and the image of a jubilant Yogi Berra leaping into Larsen's arms is now a permanent part of baseball lore. The fact that Yankees won Game 7 – and the last Subway Series with the Dodgers – is nearly an afterthought compared to Larsen's Game 5 pitching masterpiece!

Subway Series Record: Yankees 6, Dodgers 1.

New York Yankees vs. New York Giants

When the New York Highlanders set up shop in the American League in 1903, the team had high hopes that it could challenge the supremacy of the New York Giants of the National League. The Giants ruled the New York baseball scene and the team's incendiary leader, John McGraw, didn't consider the upstart Highlanders much of a threat.

Even when they weren't winning pennants, the Giants thrilled fans at the Polo Grounds with their scrappy (some said dirty), never-say-die playing style. Meanwhile, the Highlanders struggled to win some respect and draw fans to their modest ballpark, Hilltop Park.

New York Giants manager John McGraw (left) greets Connie Mack in 1911.

When a 1911 fire shut down the Polo Grounds, the Highlanders let the Giants play at Hilltop Park. A year later, when the city forced the closure of Hilltop Park, the Giants reversed the favor and offered to share the Polo Grounds with their harmless "rivals."

But within a few years, not only had the Highlanders – now called the Yankees – improved, but they were gaining loyal fans. Then the Yankees changed their fortunes and the face of baseball forever by purchasing the contract of Babe Ruth from the Boston Red Sox.

The arrival of "The Babe" shot the Yankees past the Giants in home attendance and infuriated Giants manager John McGraw. If he couldn't beat the Yankees at the gate, he would do it in the field. When the Yankees won the AL pennant in 1921, McGraw got his chance in the World Series.

Babe Ruth hits his 60th home run of the 1927 season.

The 1921 World Series was the first played entirely in one ballpark (the Polo Grounds) and the last played in the best-of-nine format.

AP/WWP

After a regular season that saw 59 homers from Ruth, 135 RBIs from Bob Meusel and 27 wins from Carl Mays, manager Miller Huggins had reason to be optimistic. But McGraw's Giants would be hard to beat, thanks to stars like "The Fordham Flash" Frankie Frisch (.341), George Kelly (122 RBI) and Art Nehf (20 wins).

Babe Ruth (right) at the Polo Grounds in 1921.

The Yankees took an early 2-0 series lead with lefty Mays and righty Waite Hoyt throwing consecutive shutouts. But the Giants smoked 20 hits in Game 3 for a 13-5 win, then evened the series with a win in Game 4. The Yanks took Game 5, but an injured Ruth would get only one at-bat the rest of the series. With Ruth on the bench, the Giants hurlers took over the last three games and spoiled the Yankees' first World Series appearance, five games to three.

The Yankees proved their success was no fluke by winning the pennant in 1922 and once again faced the Giants in the World Series. Although Ruth's numbers tailed off in the regular season, the Yankees restocked their team with their annual raid of the Red Sox roster, while the Giants trounced the National League behind Frisch (.327), Kelly (.328) and Bob Meusel's brother, Irish (132 RBI).

AP/WWP

Babe Ruth during batting practice in 1922.

Unfortunately for the Yankees, their second World Series wasn't as close as the first. The Giants won Game 1, coming from behind late on Heinie Groh's two-run single and winning 3-2. The home plate umpire declared Game 2 a 3-3 tie due to darkness (although some claimed there was still daylight left), but the Giants didn't miss a beat, shutting out the Yanks in Game 3 (3-0), and winning Games 4 and 5 by scores of 4-3 and 5-3. While Groh (.474) and Frisch (.471) torched the Yankees' pitchers in the series, Ruth's horrid .118 series average helped do the Yankees in.

But the Giants' glory days in New York came to a symbolic end in 1923. Not only did the Yankees storm to the American League pennant by 16 games, but they did it in their spectacular new home park in the

AP/WWP

Bronx, Yankee Stadium. Strangely, the Yanks had John McGraw to thank for their new park, for it was McGraw who evicted them from the Polo Grounds.

The third World Series meeting between the two rivals in 1923 looked to be no different than the others, as the Giants took Game 1 on Casey Stengel's famous, frantic inside-the-park home run in the ninth inning. But the Giants would win only one other game the rest of the way as the Yankees dominated the series, blasting

Future Yankees manager Casey Stengel in his playing days with the crosstown New York Giants.

their former landlords by scores of 8-4, 8-1 and 6-4 in the final three games. Finally, the Yankees got their money's worth out of The Babe, who hit .368 and belted three homers in the series.

By the time the Yankees and Giants met for the fourth time in the 1936 World Series, the Bronx Bombers had won four championships, while the Giants hadn't tasted glory since 1922. The Yankees didn't have the retired Ruth for this matchup, but they did have Lou Gehrig, Tony Lazzeri, Bill Dickey and superstar rookie Joe DiMaggio.

But the rejuvenated Giants, led by Carl Hubbell's 26 wins in the regular season, took the first battle from their crosstown rivals by a score of 6-1 in Game 1. Game 2 went the Bombers' way as Lazzeri hit

the second grand slam in World Series history in an 18-4 win. Two more Yankee victories pushed the Giants to the brink of elimination. Although Giants pitcher Hal Schumacher held the Yankees scoreless in Game 5, the Yankees shut the door in Game 6 with a 13-5 romp.

But the Giants were back for more in 1937 after squeaking by Chicago by two games to win the National League pennant. While both teams had 20-game winners (Red Ruffing and Lefty

Yankee catcher Bill Dickey and second basemen Tony Lazzeri before a 1936 World Series game.

Gomez for the Yankees, Cliff Melton and Carl Hubbell for the Giants), the Yankees clearly had the better bats (DiMaggio, Gehrig and Dickey drove in an astounding 459 runs combined!)

This offensive disparity spelled doom for the Giants. They got pasted by identical 8-1 scores in Games 1 and 2 (Yankees pitcher Red Ruffing drove in three runs in the latter), then dropped Game 3 by a 5-1 score.

Carl Hubbell kept the Giants alive with a 6-3 win in Game 4, but it would go for naught. Lefty Gomez shut down the Giants 4-2 in the decisive game, running his career World Series record to 5-0. By this time, even Giants fans had to admit the Subway Series train spent a lot of time parked at Yankee Stadium!

Yankee pitchers Lefty Gomez and Red Ruffing.

It would be another 14 years before the Yankees and Giants would battle for bragging rights. The Giants roared into the 1951 World Series in spectacular fashion, winning the National League pennant on Bobby Thomson's dramatic "shot heard 'round the world" home run after trailing Brooklyn by 13-1/2 games in August.

AP/WWP

Their amazing run brought them face-to-face with their postseason nemesis, the Yankees. Both teams won 98 games in 1951, and an off year by a normally potent Yankees offense gave the Giants their best subway series chance in 30 years.

Bobby Thomson's "shot heard 'round the world" home run in 1951.

As was their pattern, the Giants got off to a fast start by taking Game 1 by a 5-1 score. Highlights included Alvin Dark's three-run homer and Monte Irvin's steal of home. The Yankees bounced back as Eddie Lopat beat the Giants 3-1, but during the game Mickey Mantle tripped on a drainage cover in the outfield and suffered a knee injury that would plague him for the rest of his career.

The Giants took advantage of Mantle's absence and took Game 3, but the veteran DiMaggio mashed his eighth career World Series homer in a 6-2 Yankees win in Game 4. The bombers bludgeoned their foes 13-1 in Game 5, then sealed up another championship with a 4-3 win in Game 6, which would prove to be Joltin' Joe's last game.

AP/WWP

The Giants' Bobby Thomson is mobbed at home plate after his pennant-winning home run against the Brooklyn Dodgers.

Subway Series Record: Yankees 4, Giants 2.

The Ballparks

Yankee Stadium

Built in the Bronx, "The House That Ruth Built" opened in 1923 and quickly overtook the Polo Grounds and Ebbets Field as the preeminent ballpark in New York. Yankee Stadium ushered the home team to a World Series victory in its inaugural season. While left-handed hitters Ruth, Gehrig, Mantle and Mattingly made use of the park's short

right field porch, Maris, DiMaggio, Munson and other right-handed hitters excelled as well. Monument Park in left center field features plaques honoring Yankees greats and adds an undeniable aura of tradition. A mid-1970s renovation helped to ensure that the legacy of Yankee Stadium will march long into the new millennium.

Yankee Stadium – home of the Bronx Bombers.

Shea Stadium

Located in Flushing – within earshot of the roar of planes at LaGuardia Airport – Shea Stadium has been the home of the Mets since 1964 (the team played at the Polo Grounds for two years). Shea Stadium is named for William Shea, a New York lawyer who helped the city win an expansion team in 1962. The park has a wide-open feel, with its four decks of grandstands ending just in fair territory at each

foul line. Signature features of the park include one of the largest scoreboards in the major leagues in right field and the tremendous Big Apple that rises out of the Mets Magic Top Hat every time a Mets player hits a home run.

Fireworks erupting at Shea Stadium.

Ebbets Field

The old home of the Brooklyn Dodgers, Ebbets Field was built in 1913 in the Flatbush section of Brooklyn. The field was considered a pitcher's park until the fences were moved in the 1930s and 1940s. Memorable features of the park included a concave right field wall, Abe Stark's "Hit Sign, Win Suit" scoreboard ad and fans such as the cowbell-ringing Hilda Chester and the Dodgers Sym-Phoney Band. The park no longer stands today.

Ebbets Field in Flatbush.

Hilltop Park

The first park of the New York Yankees (then the Highlanders) was built in 1903 in Manhattan in an amazing six weeks. Typical of dead-ball era parks, Hilltop Park was cavernous, and fans were permitted to stand in the outfield. When the Polo Grounds burned down in 1911, the Yankees let the crosstown rival Giants play at Hilltop Park. The park closed in 1912 and was torn down in 1914.

Hilltop Park, home of the Highlanders.

Polo Grounds

Originally located north of Central Park in Manhattan, the Polo Grounds was built in 1883 for the New Yorks (later the Giants). The park was moved twice early in its life and its walls were constantly modified until its demolition in 1964. The park featured fair-territory bullpens and a memorial honoring major leaguer Eddie Grant, who was killed in World War I. The Yankees (1913-1922) and the Mets (1962-1963) each spent seasons at the Polo Grounds.

The famed Polo Grounds.

The 2000 Yankees
– The Year In Review

The New York Yankees headed to their spring training complex in Tampa, Florida, full of confidence. And why not? They were coming off their triumphant World Series sweep of the highly touted Atlanta Braves and they had only lost one game in twelve chances in the entire 1999 postseason.

They were winners, they were confident and they were ready . . .

But the 2000 season turned out to be quite a different season than

Reggie Jackson, Don Mattingly and Derek Jeter talk things over at spring training.

the winningest team in baseball history was accustomed to. Injuries, poor individual performances by several key players and bad breaks followed the Yankees at every turn.

The first unexpected blow came during spring training with the year-long suspension of outfielder Darryl Strawberry for cocaine use. Injuries to left fielder Shane Spencer and versatile pitcher Ramiro Mendoza during the season left Joe Torre a couple of options short. And 1999 perfect-game hurler David Cone found it exceedingly difficult just to get batters out. While the Yankees' season wasn't exactly crumbling – they were still posting W's in the win column – it sure wasn't coming easily.

Trades Turn The Tide

Throughout the beginning of the 2000 season, the Yankees lingered at or near first place, but they weren't running away from anyone. At the All-Star break, they were tied for first in the AL East standings with the Toronto Blue Jays. It was time for something drastic.

Darryl Strawberry and Joe Torre address the press during spring training.

The first of the Yankees' mid-season trades was for the Cincinnati Reds' Denny Neagle. The left-hander bolstered the Bombers' pitching rotation. The next move was arguably the most important acquisition of the season: David Justice, who came over from the Cleveland Indians. Justice became the everyday left fielder and contributed 43 runs while in the Yankees' lineup.

David Justice homers against Detroit.

Two former Yankees, Luis Polonia and Luis Sojo, also rejoined the Yankees. Sojo made an immediate contribution at second base in place of the injured Chuck Knoblauch. Designated hitters Glenallen Hill and Jose Canseco also were late-season additions. The new ingredients added to the Yankees' mix helped to put distance between the team and the other contenders for first place. The lead they built would prove to be important, as the Yankees hit a major skid in September, losing 15 of 18 games and seven in a row. The second-place Boston Red Sox couldn't catch the Yankees in the standings, however, and the Bombers went on to clinch the division.

Bring On The A's And The Division Series

As the American League Division Series between the Yankees and the AL West champion Oakland A's began, the question on everyone's mind was simple: Could the Yankees reverse the horrific tailspin that had plagued the team over the last few weeks of the regular season?

Derek Jeter and Dwight Gooden suffer another loss.

On October 4, the Yankees sent Roger Clemens to the mound Oakland in Game 1 against Gil Heredia and lost, 5-3. It looked like the Yankees' late-season woes were continuing.

Mariano Rivera turns up the heat.

Andy Pettitte proved to be the stopper for the Yankees in Game 2. Pettitte pitched 7-2/3 shutout innings and closer Mariano Rivera got the final four outs in the solid 4-0 win. The game even featured a lighthearted moment in the eighth inning when Yankees second baseman Luis Sojo got tripped up on his shoelaces and fell to the ground while trying to get a routine out. Reliever Mariano Rivera got the team out of the inning with little fanfare, and everyone could laugh easily at Sojo's faux pas.

Game 3 found the Yankees back on their home turf at Yankee Stadium. Orlando Hernandez, who didn't lose a postseason game in his rookie 1998 season or the 1999 season, continued his winning ways as he beat A's hurler Tim Hudson 4-2 and propelled the Yankees to a 2-1 lead in the series.

Roger Clemens was given the assignment of preventing a return trip to Oakland in Game 4. But Clemens and the Yankees were thumped 11-1 and Clemens now had the dubious honor of being the losing pitcher in each of the Yankees' past three postseason defeats over a two-year stretch.

With the best-of-five series now even at two games apiece, the Yankees and A's flew all the way across the country to play Game 5 the very next day in Oakland. The two-time defending champions found themselves in a do-or-die game to stay alive in the playoffs. Yankee starter Andy Pettitte only lasted into the fourth inning, but the Yankees had built a nice cushion in the first inning by scoring

Roger Clemens had his ups-and-downs in the 2000 postseason for the Yankees.

six runs, and the Yankees went on to win the game 7-5.

Next Up . . . The Mariners

The Seattle Mariners had been waiting for their next opponent after summarily sweeping the Chicago White Sox in three games in their first-round series. Yankee fans were none-too-comfortable with this

A.L.C.S. matchup, as memories of a bitter postseason defeat to the Mariners in 1995 returned.

The Yankees promptly lost Game 1 to Seattle, 2-0, despite a solid performance by Denny Neagle in his first postseason Yankees' start. The Yankees' bats were alarmingly quiet again in Game 2 and things began to look bleak. But finally, the Bombers bats erupted for seven runs in the eighth inning of Game

Andy Pettitte calls the shots on the mound. 2 to snatch a dramatic 7-1 victory.

The Yankees' momentum carried through to Game 3 at Seattle's new Safeco Field. Pettitte and the Yankees pummeled the Mariners 8-2 and took a 2-1 A.L.C.S. lead. Then, in Game 4 in Seattle, Clemens redeemed himself for some of his spotty postseason performances. He

pitched a masterful complete game, holding the Mariners to just one hit while racking up 15 strikeouts and leading the Yanks to a 5-0 win.

The Yankees looked to close out the Mariners in Game 5, but Seattle's 6-2 victory postponed the celebration, and the Yankees and their fans had to endure the agony of seeing the Mets advance to the World Series before them.

A.L.C.S. MVP David Justice sinks the Mariners in Game 6.

A Yankees win in Game 6 would mean the first Subway Series since 1956. And win they did, overcoming a 4-3 hole behind a 3-run homer by David Justice. And the Yankees charged on to the World Series, looking for a three-peat in front of their crosstown foes!

American League Champs
– The Boys From The Bronx

When the 2000 baseball season began, the Yankees were expected by most baseball observers to continue their winning ways. The roster was filled with some of the most talented players in baseball and, on top of that, these Yankees knew how to win, with three of the last four seasons culminating in world championships. But the path back to the World Series wasn't always easy. The Yankees made a series of mid-season trades to increase their offensive production and shore up their defense, and the new Yankees made an immediate contribution to the standards of excellence laid down by the team's veterans. On the following pages we take a closer look at the many stars that shine on the corner of 161st Street and River Avenue in the Bronx. Each player is listed with their uniform number, primary position, 2000 Yankees regular-season statistics and career statistics. Congratulations to the New York Yankees, the 2000 American League champions!

In each of the five years that the New York Yankees have been guided by the capable leadership of manager Joe Torre, the team has achieved the goal that every team aspires to – postseason glory. In a remarkable four of those five years, the Yankees reached the ultimate goal of a World Series appearance. Torre had managed teams before, with the Mets, Braves and Cardinals, but he never tasted the kind of success he has with the Yankees. Although there were many skeptics when Torre was brought aboard, he is now considered by many to be one of the Yankees' all-time greatest managers.

AP/WWP

Joe
Torre
6

Manager	Wins	Losses	Pctg.	Finish
2000	87	74	.540	1st, American League East champs
Career	1381	1325	.510	—

AP/WWP

AP/WWP

2 Derek **Jeter**

Outstanding. Remarkable. Unbelievable. Spectacular. How many adjectives can you come up with to describe the plays that shortstop Derek Jeter makes in the field? His .339 batting average in 2000 was nothing short of impressive, either. Jeter led his teammates in the 2000 season in batting average, hits (201) and runs (119) and he holds the Yankees' record for home runs among shortstops. Jeter, in just his fifth season, is already a respected team leader on the Yankees, despite a locker room filled with veterans. When you factor in his teen-idol good looks and his upbeat disposition, you get one winning package.

Shortstop	Avg.	AB	Hits	HR	RBI
2000	.339	593	201	15	73
Career	.322	3130	1008	78	414

Andy
Pettitte 46

Pitcher Andy Pettitte truly came into his own in the 2000 regular season for the Yankees. Fighting off the distractions of trade rumors and coming off a mediocre season in 1999, Pettitte pulled it together and put up stellar numbers in 2000. A stint on the disabled list early in the season is probably the only thing that prevented Pettitte from earning 20 wins this season. Nonetheless, Pettitte led all Pinstriper pitchers in wins with 19. Pettitte did achieve an important personal goal in the 2000 season, which was reaching 100 career victories. Not bad for a player in just his sixth major league season, all as a member of the Yankees.

Pitcher	W-L	ERA	Games	Saves	IP	K
2000	19-9	4.35	32	0	204.2	125
Career	100-55	3.99	197	0	1249	834

AP/WWP

Mariano Rivera
42

Mariano Rivera is clearly one of baseball's most intimidating relief pitchers. The woes of teams forced to face Rivera continued in the 2000 season, resulting in jammed batsmen and splintered bats. Although opposing players probably found Rivera a little more hittable than in seasons past, he continued to post impressive numbers, including 36 saves. Rivera ranks among the top players on the all-time Yankee save list – this achievement completed in just his fifth full season with the team. While his regular-season accomplishments are great, his postseason achievements are outstanding. In 2000, he broke Whitey Ford's postseason record of pitching 33 consecutive scoreless innings, and he also holds the postseason record for saves.

Pitcher	W-L	ERA	Games	Saves	IP	K
2000	7-4	2.85	66	36	75.2	58
Career	33-17	2.63	332	165	452.1	395

AP/WWP

AP/WWP

Bernie
Williams 51

Bernie Williams was just 17 years old when he signed on with the Yankees in 1985. He's learned a great deal in the last 15 years, and his achievements have been remarkable. Center field in Yankee Stadium is a lot of area to patrol, but Williams does it handily, earning three consecutive Gold Glove awards from 1997 through 1999. In the 2000 season, his 10th in pinstripes, he swung the bat well from both sides of the plate, and led his teammates in several offensive categories, including runs batted in (121), home runs (30) and triples (6). Williams also tied teammate Tino Martinez in doubles (37). These achievements added up to give the center fielder a team-leading 304 total bases and a .566 slugging percentage.

Outfield	Avg.	AB	Hits	HR	RBI
2000	.307	537	165	30	121
Career	.304	4806	1463	181	802

A utility player who can play eight defensive positions, Clay Bellinger was a very important part of the Yankees' 2000 season. With injuries to several veteran infield and outfield players, Bellinger ably stepped in around the diamond to fill in the gaps. Bellinger played in 98 games this season, and he did a terrific job coming off the bench, including hitting a game-winning solo home run in the top of the 10th inning against Texas on April 19.

Clay
Bellinger
35

Outfield	Avg.	AB	Hits	HR	RBI
2000	.207	184	38	6	21
Career	.205	229	47	7	23

Yankee fans have gotten spoiled with 1998 World Series MVP Scott Brosius patrolling the hot corner. Although his offensive production didn't come near his outrageous 1998 numbers, on defense Brosius makes the most difficult plays look easy. Whether he's diving to his left or his right to snare line drives and rob opposing players of extra-base hits or running onto the grass to grab a slow roller bare-handed, Brosius consistently makes the outs.

Scott
Brosius
18

Third Base	Avg.	AB	Hits	HR	RBI
2000	.230	470	108	16	64
Career	.254	3461	878	128	482

Designated hitter Jose Canseco was a mid-season addition to the Yankees who was claimed off waivers from Tampa Bay. Canseco became a bench player for the Yankees, an unusual position for this former American League MVP who was used to playing every day. But Canseco made the adjustment, and stepped up when he was called upon. He hit six homers for the Bombers and, despite injuries that prevented him from playing the outfield on a regular basis, put on his fielder's glove when necessary and was a true team member.

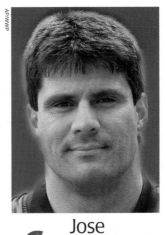

Jose
Canseco
33

Designated Hitter	Avg.	AB	Hits	HR	RBI
2000	.243	111	27	6	19
Career	.266	6801	1811	446	1358

The Rocket was red-hot this year as he compiled a 13-8 regular season record, and a team-leading 188 strikeouts. Hampered by an injury early in the season, Clemens came off the disabled list and put together a nine-game winning streak. Although he sputtered in his first two postseason starts, Clemens blew the Mariners away in the fifth game of the A.L.C.S., hurling a complete-game one-hitter and striking out 15. Clemens signed a two-year, $3.9 million contract extension in August, so look for the future Hall-of-Famer to continue blasting off for a couple more years to come.

Roger
Clemens
22

Pitcher	W-L	ERA	Games	Saves	IP	K
2000	13-8	3.70	32	0	204.1	188
Career	260-142	3.07	512	0	3666.2	3504

AP/WWP

David
Cone
36

David Cone won a Cy Young Award in 1994 with the Royals and pitched a perfect game with the Yankees against the Montreal Expos in 1999. The 2000 season, however, didn't hold any magical moments for Cone. He finished the season 4-14 and did not pull off his last three wins until August. But Cone refused to let his low winning percentage defeat him, a true sign of a Yankee warrior. His attitude never needed improvement and Cone was more than willing to face opposing batters every fifth day to prove his worth and show his mettle.

Pitcher	W-L	ERA	Games	Saves	IP	K
2000	4-14	6.91	30	0	155.0	120
Career	184-116	3.40	420	1	2745.0	2540

AP/WWP

Dwight
Gooden
17

After being released from both the Astros and the Devil Rays in 2000, Dwight "Doc" Gooden thought for sure that his major league career was over. Then his salvation came in the form of the Yankees and their pitching instructor Billy Connors, who worked with Gooden to improve his delivery. Gooden made a thrilling debut with the Yankees on July 8, pitching at Shea Stadium against the Mets. Gooden was nothing short of dramatic as he beat his former team, and earned himself a spot in the starting rotation in the place of injured Orlando Hernandez.

Pitcher	W-L	ERA	Games	Saves	IP	K
2000	4-2	3.38	18	2	64	31
Career	194-112	3.51	430	3	2800.2	2293

Middle reliever Jason Grimsley found himself in the role of emergency starter on four occasions this season with the Yankees, an interesting predicament for a pitcher who hadn't started a game since July 1996. He handled his starting assignments well, and continued to do an admirable job in his regular role coming out of the bullpen. He even picked up one save on the year.

Jason
Grimsley
38

Pitcher	W-L	ERA	Games	Saves	IP	K
2000	3-2	5.04	63	1	96.1	53
Career	28-29	5.11	219	3	597.1	385

The Cuban refugee with the unusual delivery had another respectable season with the Bombers. "El Duque" was bothered by back and elbow injuries this season, and didn't perform as well as he has in the past, but he continued to dominate opposing batters with his arsenal of pitches and funky arm motions. The postseason is a special time for Hernandez, whose nickname changes to Señor October during that time. His dominance continued in 2000 as he became the first pitcher in major league history to win his first eight postseason decisions without a loss.

Orlando
Hernandez
26

Pitcher	W-L	ERA	Games	Saves	IP	K
2000	12-13	4.51	29	0	195.2	141
Career	41-26	4.00	83	0	551.0	429

AP/WWP

Glenallen
Hill
31

Glenallen Hill was another one of those Yankees who came to the team mid-season and he contributed in a big way. He came over from the Chicago Cubs and promptly hit a home run in his first at-bat on July 24 against the Baltimore Orioles. A couple of days later, Hill was inserted into the lineup as a pinch hitter and hit a grand-slam home run to give the Yanks a 9-5 win over the Minnesota Twins. In his first month with the team, Hill hit 10 homers in 51 at bats, a feat that earned him American League Player of the Month honors for the month of August.

Designated Hitter	Avg.	AB	Hits	HR	RBI
2000	.333	132	44	16	29
Career	.273	3649	996	185	584

AP/WWP

David
Justice
28

At the end of the 2000 season, Yankee fans voted David Justice the Yankee of the Year. And for good reason. Since joining the Pinstripers on June 29 in a trade with the Cleveland Indians for Ricky Ledee, the impact Justice made on the Yankees' lineup was tremendous. In 78 games, he smacked 20 home runs and drove in 60 runs. He made opposing pitchers walk him nearly 40 times and he earned a .305 batting average. Justice's heroics continued in the A.L.C.S. as he was named Most Valuable Player in the Yankees' defeat of the Seattle Mariners.

Outfield	Avg.	AB	Hits	HR	RBI
2000	.305	275	84	20	60
Career	.283	4846	1373	276	917

Though he's only worn the Yankee pinstripes for three seasons, Chuck Knoblauch has proven to be an indispensible player. In 1999, he ranked sixth in runs scored in the American League with 120 and he has been a four-time All-Star player. Best known as a second baseman, Knoblauch has hit some rough spots with his fielding due to elbow problems but has persevered as a designated hitter for the Yankees. During his first two years wearing pinstripes, Knoblauch worked toward becoming a power hitter with 17 home runs in 1998 and 18 in 1999.

Chuck
Knoblauch
11

Second Base	Avg.	AB	Hits	HR	RBI
2000	.283	400	113	5	26
Career	.297	5545	1646	83	549

Tino Martinez has spent his five seasons with the Yankees honing his fielding skills at first base and batting his way to the top. Martinez hit at least 25 home runs and 100 RBIs per year for five seasons in a row (1995-1999), a feat that hadn't been accomplished by a Yankee since the likes of Babe Ruth, Lou Gehrig and Joe DiMaggio. He also led the team in home runs for three consecutive years between 1997 and 1999, including his personal best in 1997 with 44 home runs.

Tino
Martinez
24

First Base	Avg.	AB	Hits	HR	RBI
2000	.258	569	147	16	91
Career	.273	4774	1303	229	889

Ramiro
Mendoza
55

Hailing from Panama, pitcher Ramiro Mendoza made his major league debut with the Yankees in 1996. Mendoza was prepared to fill many roles for the Yankees in 2000, including starter, long reliever, set-up man and closer. Very few ball clubs can boast such a versatile pitcher. Unfortunately, due to tendinitis in his right shoulder, Mendoza was put on the disabled list, first in June, then again in August, and was relegated to the sidelines for the remainder of the season.

Pitcher	W-L	ERA	Games	Saves	IP	K
2000	7-4	4.25	14	0	65.2	30
Career	38-26	4.27	159	6	506.1	282

Denny
Neagle
12

The quirky Denny Neagle came to New York as part of a 2000 mid-season trade with the Cincinnati Reds. A 1996 All-Star player, his 1997 season with the Atlanta Braves featured a 20-5 record with a 2.97 ERA and he finished second in votes for the National League Cy Young Award. Besides his great record, this pitcher is also known for his good-natured pranks and his uncanny impressions of things like a train whistle and a barking dog.

Pitcher	W-L	ERA	Games	Saves	IP	K
2000	7-7	5.81	16	0	91.1	58
Career	105-69	3.92	320	3	1520.0	1144

The 6' 8" tall Jeff Nelson first put on pinstripes for the 1996 season. This right-handed pitcher is especially effective against right-handed batters and he has a deceptive sidearm pitch. This breaking ball has caused many a batter to swing and miss. The ball first appears to be headed straight for the batter who then backs away from the plate. Then it curves toward the plate, the batter takes a wild swing and usually misses. Although Nelson missed a large part of the 1999 season due to elbow surgery, this pitch has certainly served him well in the 2000 season.

Jeff Nelson
43

Pitcher	W-L	ERA	Games	Saves	IP	K
2000	8-4	2.45	73	0	69.2	71
Career	35-32	3.29	534	17	555.1	560

Yankee veteran Paul O'Neill is in his eighth season with the club and is the only player in history to play on the winning side of three perfect games (two as a member of the Yankees and one with the Cincinnati Reds). His precision throwing arm has made him a first-rate right fielder, while his batting eye has propelled him to five All-Star games. He won the American League batting title in 1994 and led the American League in hitting with men on base in 1997. O'Neill accomplished a personal milestone in 1999, as he reached 1,000 RBIs for his career.

Paul O'Neill
21

Outfield	Avg.	AB	Hits	HR	RBI
2000	.283	566	160	18	100
Career	.289	6808	1969	260	1199

Luis
Polonia
19

Luis Polonia originally played for the Bronx Bombers in 1990, 1994 and 1995 before being traded back to them from the Detroit Tigers in 2000. He spent the 1997 and 1998 seasons playing for the Mexican League and sharpening his skills. His return to the majors in 1999 was promising with a .324 batting average and career high of 10 home runs.

Outfield	Avg.	AB	Hits	HR	RBI
2000	.286	77	22	1	5
Career	.293	4840	1417	36	405

Jorge
Posada
20

2000 marks the first year that Jorge Posada has been a full-time catcher. He is in his sixth major league season, all with the Yankees. Posada has dealt well with the responsibilities of the job, having his best all-around season to date. 2000 also marked his first All-Star appearance and a caught-stealing percentage of 32.7%, which placed him third in the American League. In 1999, Posada made the record books by becoming the second catcher in history to hit a home run from both sides of the plate during the same game.

Catcher	Avg.	AB	Hits	HR	RBI
2000	.287	505	145	28	86
Career	.265	1444	382	63	231

Luis Sojo previously played for the Yankees from 1996 through 1999. In 2000, he was signed by the Pittsburgh Pirates only to come back to the Yankees later in the season. 2000 was a good year for Sojo, with two home runs for the Yankees and seven overall. Sojo played four different positions during the season: first base, second base, third base and shortstop.

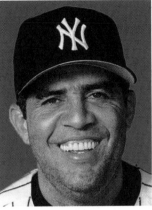

Luis
Sojo

Third Base	Avg.	AB	Hits	HR	RBI
2000	.288	125	36	2	17
Career	.264	2488	658	36	252

When Shane Spencer came up from the Yankees farm system in 1998 he made quite an impression. He ended the year with a .373 batting average and 10 home runs, and no one could wait to see what he would do with a full season in 1999. But 1999 proved to be a rocky year for Spencer with a .234 average, a stint on the disabled list and a trip back to the minor leagues. Luckily, he proved his worth to the club in 2000 by raising his batting average and doubling his RBIs. Unfortunately, Spencer suffered a season-ending injury in July.

Shane
Spencer

Outfield	Avg.	AB	Hits	HR	RBI
2000	.282	248	70	9	40
Career	.275	520	143	27	87

Stanton joined the Yankees in 1997 and has served mainly as a relief pitcher. However, in 1999, after 552 consecutive appearances as a reliever, he made his first major league start. He hit the charts with the most relief appearances before a start in the major leagues. Also in 1999, Stanton appeared in 73 games, more than any of the other Yankee pitchers, and came in second on the team with 69 games in 2000.

Mike Stanton
29

Pitcher	W-L	ERA	Games	Saves	IP	K
2000	2-3	4.10	69	0	68.0	75
Career	37-32	4.00	680	65	665.1	566

Chris Turner joined the Yankees from the Cleveland Indians in 2000 and serves as a backup catcher. He played in 37 games, one of which he played as a first baseman. He scored nine runs for the Yankees and was walked 10 times. Turner has played for four teams, including the Anaheim Angels and the Kansas City Royals, in his major league career, which started in 1993. Turner has never had more than 149 at bats or more than one home run per season.

Chris Turner
25

Catcher	Avg.	AB	Hits	HR	RBI
2000	.236	89	21	1	7
Career	.237	379	90	4	36

Jose Vizcaino has played in the major leagues for over a decade, starting with the Dodgers in 1989. After a series of trades, he returned to Los Angeles in 1998. From there, he was acquired by the Yankees during the 2000 mid-season in a trade. This versatile infielder is able to play second base, third base or shortstop and is also a switch-hitter. During his short 2000 season on the East Coast, he played 73 regular season games for the Yankees, scored 23 runs and walked 12 times.

Jose Vizcaino
13

Second Base	Avg.	AB	Hits	HR	RBI
2000	.276	174	48	0	10
Career	.269	3841	1035	21	339

Other Yankee Players

Among the many men who donned the pinstripes during the 2000 season, here are some other players worthy of a mention:

Relief pitcher **Randy Choate** made his debut in 2000, ending the season with a 4.76 ERA and a 0-1 record. Another pitcher, **Randy Keisler**, made his major league debut with the Yankees in September of 2000. Outfielder **Roberto Kelly** returned to the Yankees after an eight-year absence. He originally wore the Yankee pinstripes for six seasons, from 1987 to 1992. Left fielder **Ryan Thompson** is a former Mets player and was brought up from the Yankee farm system. Another former Mets player, **Allen Watson**, joined the Yankees as a pitcher in 1999.

Chris
Chambliss
48
Batting Coach

Not only is Chris Chambliss currently a successful batting coach, but he was also a bona fide Yankees hero as a player. He will always be remembered for his game-winning home run against the Royals in the 1976 American League Championship Series that sent the Yankees to the World Series for the first time in over a decade. He was also an All-Star in 1976 and won the Gold Glove in 1978. Chambliss ended his career in 1988 with a .279 batting average and 185 home runs.

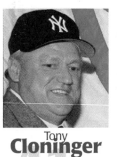

Tony
Cloninger
41
Bullpen Coach

Tony Cloninger has been the Yankees bullpen coach for several years and has quite a history himself. His biggest moment actually came as a hitter in 1966 when he made the record books by hitting two grand slams and racking up nine RBIs in the same game. As the bullpen coach, he helped the Yankees pitching staff keep their ERA the lowest or second-lowest in the American League each year between 1997 and 1999.

Lee
Mazzilli
54
First Base Coach

Former ballplayer Lee Mazzilli was a popular player for both the Mets and the Yankees and is now the first base coach for the Yanks. He began his coaching career in the Yankee farm system with their minor league teams and worked his way up. He spent a total of ten seasons with the Mets and one with the Yankees during his 14-year major league career.

Willie Randolph, the Yankees' star second baseman through the 1970s and 1980s, joined the Yankees' coaching staff in 1993. In his career as a player with the Bombers, Randolph won two World Series and four American League pennants and became team captain in 1986. He also played for the Pirates, Dodgers, A's, Brewers and Mets during his 18-year career, and compiled a lifetime .276 batting average.

Willie
Randolph

Third Base Coach

Pitching coach Mel Stottlemyre has more than 15 years of big-league coaching experience. In his pitching career with the Yankees, the only team he ever played for, he compiled a 164-139 record, which places him in the top 10 on the all-time Yankee win list. In April, Stottlemyre announced that he had cancer, and would eventually leave the team. Billy Connors, VP of player personnel and pitching instructor at the Yankees' training facility in Tampa, Florida, filled in for Stottlemyre when he left for treatment in September.

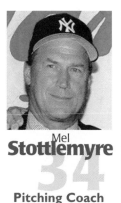

Mel
Stottlemyre

Pitching Coach

Don Zimmer has been the Yankees' bench coach for six years and has been in baseball's major leagues for more than 50 years. He has been a player, coach and manager and has been associated with nine different teams, including the Mets' inaugural 1962 season. He is the only person to be in uniform for all three Yankee perfect games – as a player for the opposing Brooklyn Dodgers in Don Larsen's game in 1956 and Yankees' bench coach for David Wells' game in 1998 and David Cone's game in 1999.

Don
Zimmer

Bench Coach

The Yankees
– Team Of The Century

1900s

Highlanders & Cellar Dwellers

New York's first and only American League team began play as the New York Highlanders at Manhattan's Hilltop Park in 1903. The franchise began as the Baltimore Orioles in 1901, but moved to New York after only two years.

Clark Griffith's plaque from the Baseball Hall of Fame.

Associated Press

In their first season in New York, the Highlanders had a respectable fourth-place finish and in 1904, they finished a competitive second. However, for most of the decade, the team showed no signs of becoming the dominant force it would later become. In fact, the cellar-dwelling 1908 team lost 103 games, an undesirable club record that still stands today.

The franchise's first New York manager was Clark Griffith, who managed the team from 1903 to part of 1908 and had a winning percentage of .531 (419-370) as the New York skipper. One of New York's finest players in their first decade was pitcher Jack Chesbro. Chesbro won 41 games in 1904, a whopping 14 wins more than the next highest single-season total in club history. Chesbro's 1904 win total is also a major league record. Another notable Highlander in the early years was Wee Willie Keeler, known for his quote, "hit 'em where they ain't." Griffith, Chesbro and Keeler each were later inducted into baseball's Hall of Fame.

Year-By-Year Records			
YEAR	PLACE	RECORD	PCTG.
1903	4th	72-62	.537
1904	2nd	92-59	.609
1905	6th	71-78	.477
1906	2nd	90-61	.596
1907	5th	70-78	.473
1908	8th	51-103	.331
1909	5th	74-77	.490
Total		520-518	.501

1910s

The Calm Before The Storm

The next decade was unremarkable for the New York franchise. The team still hadn't sniffed its first world championship, let alone an American League pennant. The team's best finish of the decade was second place in 1910, while the low point was the last-place finish of 1912.

Yankees first baseman, Wally Pipp.

For the 1913 season, the club moved from Hilltop Park to the Polo Grounds, a park they shared with the New York Giants baseball team. By this time, the team's name had gradually made a transition to the Yankees – a change that some say had to do with the fact that newspaper editors had trouble fitting the Highlanders name into headlines. In this day, the Yankees were clearly playing "second fiddle" to the powerful Giants franchise of the National League.

Year-By-Year Records			
YEAR	PLACE	RECORD	PCTG.
1910	2nd	88-63	.583
1911	6th	76-76	.500
1912	8th	50-102	.329
1913	7th	57-94	.377
1914	T-6th	70-84	.455
1915	5th	69-83	.454
1916	4th	80-74	.519
1917	6th	71-82	.464
1918	4th	60-63	.488
1919	3rd	80-59	.576
Total		701-780	.473

Some of the decade's brighter moments were provided by pitcher Bob Shawkey, first baseman Wally Pipp and shortstop Roger Peckinpaugh. When manager Miller Huggins was hired in 1918, he led the team from sixth place to fourth place in his first year. Then, in 1919, the team climbed to third. But a key moment in franchise history occurred in the off-season after the 1919 campaign when the Yankees acquired a player named Babe Ruth . . .

1920s

The First World Championships

Babe Ruth arrived from the Boston Red Sox with a jolt in 1920 and would spark the franchise to its loftiest heights yet. He made an immediate impact on his new club, smacking 54 home runs in his first year as a Yankee. That was especially amazing considering that the Yankees had hit only 45 homers *as a team* in the previous year.

Associated Press

Babe Ruth, manager Miller Huggins and Lou Gehrig.

Then, in 1921, Ruth led the Yankees to their first American League pennant. Awaiting them in the World Series were none other than their Polo Grounds counterparts, the New York Giants. The Yankees lost that series 5 games to 3 in the last World Series played with a best-of-nine format. In 1922, the Yankees and Giants again duked it out in the World Series, and this time the Giants swept the Yankees 4 games to none.

The Yankees were defeated, but they kept on fighting. In 1923, they moved into Yankee Stadium, their brand new ballpark in the Bronx. Home at last! Once again, the Yankees and Giants won their respective league titles, and faced off in the World Series for the third consecutive season. This time, the Yankees took care of business. By beating the Giants 4 games to 2, the Yankees christened their new stadium with the franchise's first world championship.

It took the Yankees three years after that first championship to return to the

Year-By-Year Records			
YEAR	PLACE	RECORD	PCTG.
1920	3rd	95-59	.617
1921	1st	98-55	.641
1922	1st	94-60	.610
1923	1st	98-54	.645
1924	2nd	89-63	.586
1925	7th	69-85	.448
1926	1st	91-63	.591
1927	1st	110-44	.714
1928	1st	101-53	.656
1929	2nd	88-66	.571
Total		933-602	.608

Red denotes World Series title

World Series. Meanwhile, in 1925, first baseman Lou Gehrig began his streak of playing in 2,130 consecutive games. When the Yankees reached the World Series in 1926, they faced a new opponent, the St. Louis Cardinals. The Cardinals came from behind in the series to edge the Yankees 4-3. The dramatic series was highlighted by a Babe Ruth power display in Game 4, when he bashed three home runs.

When baseball fans discuss the "greatest teams ever," the 1927 Yankees are often at the top of the list. The fearsome lineup, including Ruth, Gehrig, outfielder Bob Meusel and second baseman Tony Lazzeri, was commonly referred to as the "Murderers' Row" and the strong pitching staff was led by Waite Hoyt. Ruth hit 60 home runs in 1927, a major league record that would stand until 1961. And the powerful Yankees swept the Pittsburgh Pirates in the World Series to win their second championship.

Associated Press

Babe Ruth, with baseball commissioner Kenesaw Mountain Landis and Yankee teammate Bob Meusel in 1922.

The Yankees followed that up with another World Series sweep in 1928 – this time against the St. Louis Cardinals, avenging the 1926 World Series defeat.

For the decade, the Yankees team averaged an incredible 93 victories per year and won 110 games in 1927. Manager Miller Huggins passed away late in the 1929 season, leaving a legacy as one of the Yankees' all-time great managers and the skipper who led the team during their rise to prominence.

World Series History

YEAR	OPPONENT	RESULT
1921	New York Giants	L, 3-5
1922	New York Giants	L, 0-4
1923	New York Giants	W, 4-2
1926	St. Louis Cardinals	L, 3-4
1927	Pittsburgh Pirates	W, 4-0
1928	St. Louis Cardinals	W, 4-0

Four-In-A-Row!

By this time, the Yankees were developing a real taste for world championships. The Yankees finished first five times during the 1930s,

Associated Press

Joe DiMaggio in the minors, one season before his Yankees debut.

and went on to win the World Series each time, including an unprecedented four-in-a-row to close out the decade. Manager Joe McCarthy joined the Yankees in 1931 and led the team through some of its greatest years.

Babe Ruth and Lou Gehrig continued to drive the Yankees' success. In a 1932 regular-season game against Philadelphia, Gehrig became the first major league player to hit four home runs in a game.

The Yankees strung together 107 victories in 1932 to win another trip to the World Series. The 4-0 dismantling of the Chicago Cubs is best known for Babe Ruth's "called shot" home run in Game 3 when, legend has it, he pointed to the outfield stands, then promptly crushed a home run over the center field wall.

Babe Ruth's final season was in 1934, and he finished his career with 714 home runs (a record only eclipsed by Hank Aaron). The Yankees were rejuvenated in 1936 by the arrival of outfielder Joe DiMaggio. DiMaggio went on to have an wonderful career with the Yankees, picking up numerous admirers (like Marilyn Monroe) and nicknames (including "Joltin' Joe" and "The Yankee Clipper") along the way.

Year-By-Year Records

YEAR	PLACE	RECORD	PCTG.
1930	3rd	86-68	.558
1931	2nd	94-59	.614
1932	1st	107-47	.695
1933	2nd	91-59	.607
1934	2nd	94-60	.610
1935	2nd	89-60	.597
1936	1st	102-51	.667
1937	1st	102-52	.662
1938	1st	99-53	.651
1939	1st	106-45	.702
Total		970-554	.636

Red denotes World Series title

The 1936 team was led by Gehrig and DiMaggio, along with pitchers Lefty Gomez and Red Ruffing, outfielder George Selkirk and catcher Bill Dickey. In the 1936 World Series, the Yankees and New York Giants met in the Fall Classic for the first time since 1923. The Giants' star pitcher Carl Hubbell was a tough nemesis for the Bronx Bombers, but the Yankees prevailed 4 games to 2.

Associated Press

Bill Dickey, Lou Gehrig, Joe DiMaggio and Tony Lazzeri.

In 1937, the Yankees once again found themselves face-to-face with Hubbell and the Giants in the World Series. The Yankees dispatched the Giants 4-1 in the series, giving the Yankees three wins in the five World Series meetings thus far in this heated intracity rivalry.

The 1938 Yankees were again led by DiMaggio and Gehrig (though the venerable first baseman's stats had begun to slip), along with rookie second baseman Joe Gordon. The Yankees swept the Chicago Cubs in the World Series for the second time in the decade.

The 1939 season was an emotional roller coaster for the Yankees. First, in early 1939, legendary Yankees owner Colonel Jacob Ruppert died. Then, Lou Gehrig, nicknamed the "Iron Horse" because of his amazing consecutive-game streak, struggled at the beginning of the season. Afraid he was hurting the team, Gehrig finally asked to sit out a game, ending his streak at 2,130 games.

World Series History

YEAR	OPPONENT	RESULT
1932	Chicago Cubs	W, 4-0
1936	New York Giants	W, 4-2
1937	New York Giants	W, 4-1
1938	Chicago Cubs	W, 4-0
1939	Cincinnati Reds	W, 4-0

Something seemed to be wrong with Gehrig's health, and he was soon diagnosed with a rare and deadly disease that became known as

"Lou Gehrig's Disease." Gehrig's career came to an abrupt end. On July 4, 1939, "Lou Gehrig Appreciation Day" was held at Yankee Stadium and Gehrig said goodbye to his teammates, both past and present, and the fans of New York. In his speech, the dying Gehrig declared himself "the luckiest man on the face of the earth" – a powerful and emotional moment that has lodged itself permanently in baseball lore. Gehrig passed away two years later in 1941.

Associated Press

Lou Gehrig and Babe Ruth at Yankee Stadium on "Lou Gehrig Appreciation Day."

The Yankees, despite the sudden retirement of Gehrig during the regular season, pulled it together in 1939 to win another American League pennant, winning 106 games. The Yankees steamrolled the Cincinnati Reds in the World Series 4-0 for their fourth consecutive world championship.

> "Fans, for the past two weeks you have been reading about the bad break I got. Yet today I consider myself the luckiest man on the face of the earth."
>
> *– excerpt from Lou Gehrig's emotional farewell speech on July 4, 1939*

Joltin' Joe DiMaggio

The Yankees' dynasty was well-established by the 1940s and the new generation of players made sure that the legacy begun by Ruth and Gehrig would continue. Although their streak of four consecutive world championships came to an end in 1940, the Yankees still won four more World Series titles during the decade. The Yankees were now Joe DiMaggio's team, although second baseman Joe Gordon, outfielder Charlie Keller and shortstop Phil Rizzuto also played key roles in the 1940s.

Associated Press

Joe DiMaggio strokes another hit during his record hitting streak in 1941.

In 1941, the Yankees charged to another American League pennant, proving that the team's third-place finish in 1940 was just a fluke. In the 1941 World Series, the Yankees faced their neighbors from a couple boroughs to the south – the Brooklyn Dodgers – for the first time. The Yankees beat the Dodgers 4-1, in a series that featured a heartbreaking Game 4 for Dodgers fans when Brooklyn's catcher Mickey Owen dropped a third strike with two outs in the ninth inning to help the Yankees steal the victory.

The 1941 season was notable for an amazing individual accomplishment during the regular season that still stands as a major league record today. Joe DiMaggio began a consecutive-game hitting streak on May 15, 1941 that continued on through the rest of May, all of June and into July – 56 games in a row with a hit!

Year-By-Year Records

YEAR	PLACE	RECORD	PCTG.
1940	3rd	88-66	.571
1941	1st	101-53	.656
1942	1st	103-51	.669
1943	1st	98-56	.636
1944	3rd	83-71	.539
1945	4th	81-71	.533
1946	3rd	87-67	.565
1947	1st	97-57	.630
1948	3rd	94-60	.610
1949	1st	97-57	.630
Total		929-609	.604

Red denotes World Series title

The 1942 baseball season began with World War II in full swing. Despite the distractions of the country being at war, the Yankees put together their highest victory total of the decade, 103 wins. But the St. Louis Cardinals, led by Stan Musial and Enos Slaughter, defeated the Yankees in the World Series 4-1. The Yankees and their fans were not accustomed to losing in the World Series, and during the off-season, they had to deal with another loss – Joe DiMaggio (in addition to other top players) left the Yankees to join the war effort.

Associated Press

Joe McCarthy, Yankees manager.

In 1943, a ragtag band of Yankees kept up the team's rich tradition by beating up on the rest of the war-depleted league. After winning the American League pennant, the Yankees again found the St. Louis Cardinals waiting for them in the World Series. The Yankees turned the tables on the Cardinals with a 4-1 series win of their own.

The rest of the war years were lean years for the Yankees. Finally, Joe DiMaggio and the rest of the stars returned from the war in 1946, but the Yankees were dealt a setback when legendary manager Joe McCarthy resigned. The Yankees could only muster a third-place finish, as the hated Boston Red Sox advanced to the World Series, led by one of Joe DiMaggio's biggest rivals of the era, Ted Williams. A bright spot in the 1946 season was the arrival of Yogi Berra, who would go on to become one of baseball all-time greatest catchers.

The Yankees returned to power in 1947, winning the American League pennant and

World Series History		
YEAR	OPPONENT	RESULT
1941	Brooklyn Dodgers	W, 4-1
1942	St. Louis Cardinals	L, 1-4
1943	St. Louis Cardinals	W, 4-1
1947	Brooklyn Dodgers	W, 4-3
1949	Brooklyn Dodgers	W, 4-1

then engaging the crosstown Brooklyn Dodgers in a classic World Series encounter. In Game 4, the feisty Dodgers broke up a no-hit bid by the Yankees' Bill Bevens with two outs in the ninth inning and pulled out a dramatic victory. Then, in Game 6, Brooklyn outfielder Al

Gionfriddo robbed Joe DiMaggio of a home run, preserving another Dodgers victory. The Yankees, who hadn't played in a do-or-die World Series Game 7 since losing to the Cardinals in 1926, refused to fold. With a 5-2 victory in Game 7, the Yankees won their 11th world championship.

Joe DiMaggio crosses the plate after hitting a home run in Game 3 of the 1947 World Series.

The Yankees had another good season in 1948, but they were denied the American League pennant in a close race with Cleveland and Boston. The Yankees began the 1949 season with a new manager. His name was Casey Stengel, and he would follow in the footsteps of Miller Huggins and Joe McCarthy as one of the greatest Yankee managers ever. Stengel proved his managerial mettle right away, as he guided the Yankees through a difficult stretch of the 1949 season without the injured Joe DiMaggio. Bolstered by a strong pitching staff that included Allie Reynolds, Vic Raschi and Eddie Lopat, the Yankees battled their way to the World Series. For the third time in the decade, the Brooklyn Dodgers were the Yankees' opponents in the World Series. And for the third time, the Yankees emerged victorious, winning the series 4-1.

Casey Stengel and his team celebrate their 1949 World Series win.

As the Yankees approached the halfway point of the century, their position as a baseball dynasty had already been firmly clinched. In the past 29 seasons, they had won 16 American League pennants and 12 World Series titles. And, as it turned out, the Yankees weren't done.

1950s

A Decade Like No Other

Picking up from 1949, the Yankees continued a run of nine American League pennants in ten years. And in a bizarre irony, when they dropped to second place in 1954, the team had 103 wins and the best regular-season record of the entire 10-year stretch!

Associated Press

Whitey Ford leaves the Army and re-joins the Yankees.

In 1950, the Yankees' great pitching staff got even better when Whitey Ford joined the rotation. The season ended with a World Series matchup against the Philadelphia Phillies, who barely put up a fight in losing the series 4 games to none. Ford, the rookie sensation, won the series' deciding game.

The 1951 regular season was highlighted by Allie Reynolds' two no-hitters against Cleveland and Boston. The Yankees went to the World Series again that year, and there they renewed an acquaintance with an old crosstown rival, the New York Giants, who featured a rookie outfielder named Willie Mays. The Yankees had seemingly left their once-dominant Giant counterparts in the dust back in the 1920s, but the Giants came into the series with a burst of momentum following Bobby Thompson's pennant-winning home run against the Brooklyn Dodgers. The Giants won two of the first three games in the series, but eventually fell to the Yankees 4-2.

The Yankees franchise seemed to have an uncanny knack for having a new

Year-By-Year Records

YEAR	PLACE	RECORD	PCTG.
1950	1st	98-56	.636
1951	1st	98-56	.636
1952	1st	95-59	.617
1953	1st	99-52	.656
1954	2nd	103-51	.669
1955	1st	96-58	.623
1956	1st	97-57	.630
1957	1st	98-56	.636
1958	1st	92-62	.597
1959	3rd	79-75	.513
Total		955-582	.621

Red denotes World Series title

superstar emerge just as an aging legend was ready to call it quits. A talented, young outfielder named Mickey Mantle joined the team during the 1951 season. At the end of the same season, the great Joe DiMaggio, the "Yankee Clipper," retired from the game.

Associated Press

Mickey Mantle in 1951.

It was getting to the point where the Yankees were pretty much expected to be the American League representatives in the World Series each year. And in the 1940s and 1950s, there was also a good chance that the National League team would hail from New York as well. In 1952, it was the Brooklyn Dodgers who returned to face the three-time defending champions in the World Series. The Dodgers were an explosive team that featured the likes of Jackie Robinson and Duke Snider. The Yankees edged the Dodgers, 4-3, to win their fourth straight world championship.

The boys from Brooklyn and the Bronx met again in the 1953 World Series. Surely, the Dodgers were getting tired of battling all year long, just to lose to their crosstown neighbors each year. Though the series was tied at two games apiece after Game 4, the Yankees took the series 4-2, with the help of some key contributions from second baseman Billy Martin. The 1953 title was the Yankees' fifth consecutive world championship, a feat that surpassed even the incredible streak of the 1936-39 Yankees.

The next year, in 1954, the Yankees posted a tremendous 103-51 regular-season record. Amazingly, it wasn't good enough, as the Cleveland Indians won 111 games to grab the American League pennant. Things seemed to return to normal again in 1955, when the

World Series History		
YEAR	OPPONENT	RESULT
1950	Philadelphia Phillies	W, 4-0
1951	New York Giants	W, 4-2
1952	Brooklyn Dodgers	W, 4-3
1953	Brooklyn Dodgers	W, 4-2
1955	Brooklyn Dodgers	L, 3-4
1956	Brooklyn Dodgers	W, 4-3
1957	Milwaukee Braves	L, 3-4
1958	Milwaukee Braves	W, 4-3

Yankees and Dodgers won their respective pennants. Everything seemed to be going according to script as the Yankees won the first two

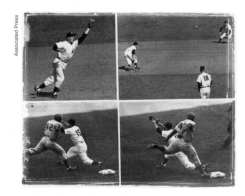

games of the World Series, but with help from Roy Campanella and Gil Hodges, the determined Dodgers stormed back and captured the series 4-3.

Try as they might, the Dodgers can't get a hit off of Don Larsen in the 1956 World Series.

In 1956, the Yankees and Dodgers were at it again in the World Series for the seventh time in less than two decades. No one knew at the time that this would actually be the last time that two New York teams would meet in the World Series for 44 years! And the two teams produced another classic, highlighted in Game 5 by the only perfect game (no Dodgers reached base) in World Series history, pitched by the Yankees' Don Larsen. The series was extended to seven games for the second year in a row, but this time it was the Yankees who came out victorious.

The Yankees continued their dominance for the next two seasons. In both 1957 and 1958, the American League champion Yankees battled the Milwaukee Braves (who would later move to Atlanta and become a 1990s-era rival of both the Yankees and the Mets) in the World Series. Both times, the series was extended to a seventh and deciding game. The Braves, who featured the dominating pitcher Warren Spahn and future home run king Hank Aaron, bested the Yankees in the 1957 series 4-3. But the Yankees came back in 1958 to beat the Braves 4-3, marking the final world championship under manager Casey Stengel.

Yogi Berra hugs Don Larsen at the end of his perfect game achievement.

Mantle And Maris

The 1960s were a decade of great highs and surprising lows for the Yankees. The team began the decade with five consecutive World Series appearances, but in the second half of the decade they found themselves in the unfamiliar position of being out of contention.

Associated Press

Yogi Berra lunges for a catch.

The Yankees won the American League pennant in 1960 and moved on to the World Series against the Pittsburgh Pirates. The 1960 eries featured one of the most memorable moments in postseason history – unfortunately a moment that most Yankee fans would prefer to forget. The Yankees, paced by stars such as Mickey Mantle, Roger Maris, Yogi Berra and Elston Howard, were an offensive juggernaut and several of the games in the series were lopsided Yankees victories. But the Pirates pushed the series to a deciding seventh game and that's when Pittsburgh second baseman Bill Mazeroski made history. It was the bottom of the ninth inning and the ballgame was tied at 9 runs apiece. Mazeroski hit a dramatic home run off Yankee pitcher Ralph Terry – becoming the first player in history to end a World Series with a home run.

Manager Casey Stengel left the team after the 1960 season and Ralph Houk became the new skipper in 1961. But that's not the only reason why the number "61" has become etched in New York Yankee history.

Year-By-Year Records

YEAR	PLACE	RECORD	PCTG.
1960	1st	97-57	.630
1961	1st	109-53	.673
1962	1st	96-66	.593
1963	1st	104-57	.646
1964	1st	99-63	.611
1965	6th	77-85	.475
1966	10th	70-89	.440
1967	9th	72-90	.444
1968	5th	83-79	.512
1969	5th	80-81	.497
Total		887-720	.552

Red denotes World Series title

Under Houk's tutelage, the Yankees terrorized the American League in 1961, winning 109 games in the regular season. But the season was highlighted by the home run prowess of Yankee teammates Mickey Mantle and Roger Maris. Both sluggers were approaching Babe Ruth's hallowed home run record of 60 in a season. It was Maris who emerged as baseball's new single-season home run king when he bashed his 61st home run on the final day of the regular season (Mantle finished with 54).

The powerful Yankees surged into the 1961 World Series against the Cincinnati Reds. The Yankees had developed a troubling postseason habit – their five most recent World Series appearances had each gone a full seven games. This time, the Yankees left nothing to chance and turned away the Reds 4-1.

Associated Press

Roger Maris and Mickey Mantle in 1961.

The next two seasons featured World Series matchups between the Yankees and two familiar opponents, the Giants in 1962 and the Dodgers in 1963. But this was different, as both teams had now relocated to California. The Yankees defeated the San Francisco Giants 4-3 in 1962 to record the 20th world championship for the storied franchise. However, in the 1963 World Series against the Los Angeles Dodgers, the Yankees were shut down by pitchers Sandy Koufax, Johnny Podres and Don Drysdale and were on the losing end of a 4-0 sweep.

The Yankees made their final postseason appearance of the decade against the St. Louis Cardinals in 1964. The Yankees, now managed by former star catcher Yogi Berra, gave the Bob Gibson–led Cardinals a battle, but eventually lost 4-3.

After the 1964 season, Yogi Berra left as manager and for the rest of the decade, the Yankees finished no higher than 5th place.

World Series History

YEAR	OPPONENT	RESULT
1960	Pittsburgh Pirates	L, 3-4
1961	Cincinnati Reds	W, 4-1
1962	San Francisco Giants	W, 4-3
1963	Los Angeles Dodgers	L, 0-4
1964	St. Louis Cardinals	L, 3-4

1970s

Steinbrenner Stirs Up The Bronx

By 1970, the aura that had surrounded the Yankees franchise for nearly 50 years seemed in jeopardy of fading away. The great Yankee

New owner George Steinbrenner.

stars of the 1960s – Mickey Mantle, Whitey Ford and Roger Maris – were no longer in the league and manager Ralph Houk was in the midst of his second, and less successful, tour of duty with the club. Even the hapless crosstown Mets, who had just been formed in 1962, had somehow walked away with the 1969 World Series title.

But the Yankees were due for a turn-around, and the seeds of rebirth were planted in 1973, when a brazen businessman named George Steinbrenner bought the team. Steinbrenner brought an intense desire for excellence to the organization and was willing to spend whatever it would take to build a winner.

From very early on, Steinbrenner displayed a penchant for changing managers almost at will. In the 1970s, the club was led by Houk, Bill Virdon, Billy Martin, Bob Lemon and then back to Billy Martin. The stormy relationship between Steinbrenner and Martin was highly publicized, but it was during Martin's tenure that the pride of the Yankees was restored to its former glory.

The Yankees won the American League East division in 1976, then defeated the Kansas City Royals in the American League Championship Series to return to the World Series for the first time in over a decade. The team's roster was loaded with

Year-By-Year Records

YEAR	PLACE	RECORD	PCTG.
1970	2nd	93-69	.574
1971	4th	82-80	.506
1972	4th	79-76	.510
1973	4th	80-82	.494
1974	2nd	89-73	.549
1975	3rd	83-77	.519
1976	1st	97-62	.610
1977	1st	100-62	.617
1978	1st	100-63	.613
1979	4th	89-71	.556
Total		892-715	.555

Red denotes World Series title

talent, including catcher Thurman Munson, pitcher Catfish Hunter, first baseman Chris Chambliss and third baseman Graig Nettles. The Yankees met the defending world champion Cincinnati Reds in the 1976 World Series. The Yankees were no match for the "Big Red Machine," as Cincinnati was referred to at the time, and were swept 4 games to none.

Associated Press

Reggie Jackson at the plate.

Not satisfied with just getting to the World Series, the Yankees were on a mission in 1977 to bring another world championship to the Bronx. For Steinbrenner, that meant opening his wallet – and he signed the gregarious slugger Reggie Jackson before the season. The 1977 club, led by pitcher Ron Guidry, reliever Sparky Lyle and a potent offense, won 100 games during the regular season.

Again, the Yankees held off the Kansas City Royals in the American League Championship Series and moved on to face the Los Angeles Dodgers in the 1977 World Series. Reggie Jackson helped power the Yankees to their 21st world championship with five home runs in the series. Jackson cemented his reputation as "Mr. October" with three home runs in three consecutive at-bats in the decisive sixth game of the series.

Billy Martin was replaced by Bob Lemon as manager in mid-season 1978, but the Yankees still won 100 games for the second straight year. At the end of the regular season, the Yankees were tied for first place with the Boston Red Sox. A one-game playoff was held at Boston's Fenway Park to determine the division champion. The Yankees earned a dramatic victory, helped by a three-run homer by light-hitting shortstop Bucky Dent. The Yankees went on to win their second consecutive World Series title by defeating the same opponents as the previous year: the Kansas City Royals in the A.L.C.S., then the Los Angeles Dodgers for the crown.

World Series History

YEAR	OPPONENT	RESULT
1976	Cincinnati Reds	L, 0-4
1977	Los Angeles Dodgers	W, 4-2
1978	Los Angeles Dodgers	W, 4-2

The Lost Decade

Bob Watson and Steve Yeager in Game 4 of the 1981 World Series.

The 1980s were a lackluster decade for the Yankees (by their high standards) that were perhaps more notable for Steinbrenner's continuous manager-shuffling than for on-the-field successes. The team did win the American League East in 1980 under manager Dick Howser, but the law of averages caught up with the Yankees when they faced the Kansas City Royals in the A.L.C.S. for the fourth time in five seasons. The Royals swept the series, avenging three bitter defeats in the 1970s.

In 1981, the Yankees (with new outfielder Dave Winfield) were in first place when a players' strike hit the league. The players later returned, and the winners of both "halves" of the season were awarded berths in postseason play. The Yankees won two playoff series (against the Milwaukee Brewers and the Oakland A's) to advance to the World Series against the Los Angeles Dodgers, but lost 4-2.

The Yankees were led in the latter half of the 1980s by first baseman Don Mattingly and outfielder Rickey Henderson, but the decade came to a close with no Yankee world championships for the first time since the 1910s.

World Series History

YEAR	OPPONENT	RESULT
1981	Los Angeles Dodgers	L, 2-4

Year-By-Year Records

YEAR	PLACE	RECORD	PCTG.
1980	1st	103-59	.636
1981	1st	34-22	.607
	6th	25-26	.490
1982	5th	79-83	.488
1983	3rd	91-71	.562
1984	3rd	87-75	.537
1985	2nd	97-64	.602
1986	2nd	90-72	.556
1987	4th	89-73	.549
1988	5th	85-76	.528
1989	5th	74-87	.460
Total		854-708	.547

Return To The Top

The 1990s were a wild ride for the New York Yankees and their fans. The decade began with a couple of the worst seasons in the history of the franchise. Then, in 1994, the Yankees put together a championship-caliber season for manager Buck Showalter, only to have a player's strike bring the season to a halt and leave the team dangling in first place, with their dreams of glory unfulfilled.

Associated Press

First baseman Don Mattingly.

In 1995, the Yankees finished second in the American League East, but they qualified for the playoffs as a wild card in a new system that required two playoff rounds before reaching the World Series. The Yankees, despite a dramatic extra-inning home run by Jim Leyritz in Game 2, lost an exciting best-of-five series to the Seattle Mariners, who were led by outfielder Ken Griffey Jr. and pitcher Randy Johnson.

The 1995 season marked the end of Don Mattingly's fine career. Sadly, the team's classy leader throughout the late 1980s and early 1990s never played in a World Series game with a franchise whose name is synonymous with world championships.

Manager Buck Showalter also left the Yankees at the end of the 1995 campaign, and George Steinbrenner surprised some observers by hiring Joe Torre to replace him. Torre had a distinguished playing career and had previous managing stints

Year-By-Year Records

YEAR	PLACE	RECORD	PCTG.
1990	7th	67-95	.414
1991	5th	71-91	.438
1992	T-4th	76-86	.469
1993	2nd	88-74	.543
1994	1st	70-43	.619
1995	2nd	79-65	.549
1996	1st	92-70	.568
1997	2nd	96-66	.593
1998	1st	114-48	.704
1999	1st	98-64	.605
Total		851-702	.548

Red denotes World Series title

with the New York Mets, Atlanta Braves and St. Louis Cardinals, but he was saddled with a losing record for his managerial career. But Joe Torre proved the skeptics wrong.

At the core of the 1996 Yankees were players such as outfielders Bernie Williams and Paul O'Neill and pitcher David Cone. Among the

Associated Press

newcomers in 1996 were first baseman Tino Martinez, who was acquired from Seattle to fill Mattingly's formidable shoes, and rookies Derek Jeter at shortstop and Mariano Rivera in the bullpen. The team banded together to win the Yankees' first world championship since 1978, efficiently disposing of the Texas Rangers, Baltimore

Derek Jeter added pop to the Yankees' lineup at the shortstop position.

Orioles and Atlanta Braves in the postseason. The baseball world was put on notice – the Yankees were back.

In 1997, the defending champion Yankees returned to the postseason as the wild card, but lost to the Cleveland Indians in a first-round playoff series. This proved to be a temporary setback for the Yankees, as they roared back in 1998 with an American League–record 114 wins during the regular season. In the postseason, the Yankees swept the Rangers 3-0, defeated the Indians 4-2, then swept the San Diego Padres 4-0 to win the 1998 World Series title.

The Yankees looked to repeat in 1999 and again they won the division title. The Yankees swept the Rangers in the first round of the playoffs, which set up a historic matchup with the Boston Red Sox in the A.L.C.S. Despite losing to Boston ace Pedro Martinez in Game 3, the Yankees won the series 4-1. Then, in a World Series sweep, the Yankees dismantled the Atlanta Braves for the second time in four years – bringing an amazing 25th world championship to the Bronx. At the close of the 1990s, the Yankees could undisputably claim the title of "Team Of The Century."

World Series History		
YEAR	OPPONENT	RESULT
1996	Atlanta Braves	W, 4-2
1998	San Diego Padres	W, 4-0
1999	Atlanta Braves	W, 4-0

The 2000 *Mets*
– The Year In Review
A Second-Place Success Story

Associated Press

Derek Bell is cheered for his game-winning home run.

Associated Press

Mike Hampton in the dugout.

For the past two seasons, the Mets had been faced with being in the wrong place at the wrong time. The place was the National League East and the time was an era of dominance by the Atlanta Braves that saw the Braves win the division eight times over the past nine years.

Would 2000 finally be the Mets year? Or would they again be swatted away by the reigning powerhouse of the National League? All of the pieces seemed to be in place for a Mets triumph. They had won 97 games in 1999 before falling to Atlanta in the National League Championship Series. They had the best-hitting catcher in the game. But there were still many unanswered questions plaguing the team as they prepared for the first season of the new millennium. Did they have enough starting pitching? Would the bullpen hold up? Would they *ever* get the best of the Braves?

In the off-season, the Mets maneuvered to get ace pitcher Mike Hampton from the Astros in a trade that also included outfielder Derek Bell. These two acquisitions would pay out great dividends for the Mets over the season.

After an April matchup against the Los Angeles Dodgers was postponed due to snow, the Mets had to wonder if their season was already snowballing out of control. Their slow start left them at the bottom of the NL East, and Mike Hampton, who had arrived from Houston with much fanfare, was 0-3.

Although the Mets were 48-38 at the All-Star break, there was still room for improvement. As the second half of the season began, the Mets were ready to make their push for the pennant. Shortstop Mike Bordick

Timo Perez, a Mets fan favorite in the 2000 postseason.

was acquired from the Baltimore Orioles to solidify the hole left by Rey Ordonez's absence from the lineup due to a broken arm.

Perhaps the wisest decision made by the Mets was the acquisition of not a big-name superstar, but rather a young minor league outfielder named Timoniel Perez. Although Perez would only play in 24 regular-season games for Mets, his flurry of postseason hits had fans chanting "Timo! Timo! Timo!" at Shea Stadium in the fall.

The Mets had many hot stretches in the second half of the season, the most impressive being a stretch of 22 games in which they won 18. As August came to a close, the Mets actually found themselves tied with the Braves in the NL East. The Braves exhibited their characteristic tenacity, refusing to relinquish their lead in the division. The Mets faded in their attempt to catch Atlanta, but New York took solace in clinching a playoff berth. Although as the wild card team the Mets would have to face the team with the best record in the National League, there must have been some relief that it was not the Braves this year.

The Giant Killers

The San Francisco Giants possessed the best record in the major leagues with 97 wins. Their potent offense, led by Barry

Pitchers Rick Reed and Bobby Jones celebrate the Mets' wild card berth.

Bonds and Jeff Kent, had bombed the Mets with an incredible 46 runs during the regular season, including a shocking four-game sweep in May. In a best-of-five series, the old adage "anything can happen" is appropriate. Anything can, and definitely did, happen in the opening round of playoffs between these two teams.

The Mets split the first two games with the Giants on the road at Pacific Bell Park. Offense was the name of the game in Games 1 and

Mike Hampton pitches in Game 1 of the National League Division Series against San Francisco.

2. San Francisco's ability to hit the long ball was vividly displayed by Ellis Burks' three-run homer off of Mets' starter Mike Hampton, who had previously held a 9-0 lifetime record against San Francisco going into the game.

While Game 2 didn't exactly offer a return to form for the Mets, they were able to survive a three-run homer from J.T. Snow and eventually gutted out victory in a 10-inning effort.

Game 3 supplied even more extra-inning excitement. Benny Agbayani sent Mets fans home happy with a game-winning home run off of Aaron Fultz in the bottom of the 13th, giving the Mets a 2-1 Divisional Series lead in the best-of-five series.

Outfielder Benny Agbayani hits a "walk-off" home run to end Game 3 against the Giants.

In a series that seemed to rest on which team could send the ball out of the yard fastest and farthest, the deciding game was won on the principle that good pitching always beats out good hitting. The "good pitching" was supplied by Bobby Jones, who proved to be nearly unhittable. Thanks to an optimal performance from Jones, as well as timely hits from Robin Ventura and Edgardo Alfonzo, the Mets were awarded their second consecutive trip to the National League Championship Series.

Victory Is In The Cards

Over the past decade, it has seemed that the road to the Fall Classic always passed through Atlanta. But with the St. Louis Cardinals

sweeping the Braves in their playoff series, Mets fans had reason to believe that this would be the year that their team would prove to be unstoppable.

The Mets performed the tough task of winning the first two games against the Cards on the road. Mike Hampton pitched well in the Game 1 win, and Al Leiter also turned in a solid pitching effort in a Game 2 start.

Any thoughts of a sweep were swept away as St. Louis beat the Mets

The Mets rejoice after winning the N.L.D.S.

8-2 at Shea Stadium. Andy Benes kept the Mets under control, and Mets pitcher Rick Reed exhibited little control, as he got lit up for five runs over 3-1/3 innings.

The Mets rebounded in Game 4, finding themselves on the winning end of a 10-6 slugfest. A new L.C.S. record was set when the Mets

smashed five doubles in the first inning, including four consecutive two-baggers. The Mets' date with destiny was decided in Game 5, with pitcher Mike Hampton blanking the Cardinals 7-0. Hampton was named Most Valuable Player of the N.L.C.S., thanks to his 16 scoreless innings over the course of the series.

For the first time since 1986, the Mets didn't have to look forward to next year. Their moment in

Hampton shut down the Cardinals in Game 5 and he was named the series' MVP.

the sun was now. The Mets were National League champions, and just a subway ride away from the World Series.

National League Champs
The Kings From Queens

The New York Mets' 1999 season ended in the National League Championship Series, just two victories short of a potential matchup in the World Series with the New York Yankees. Despite the disappointing end to 1999, the Mets and their fans had reasons to be excited about their chances in 2000 campaign. Most of the key players were back, and now they had quality postseason experience under their belts. Though a few important players left in the offseason (including Roger Cedeno and Octavio Dotel to the Astros and John Olerud to the Mariners), the Mets picked up solid veterans such as Mike Hampton, Derek Bell and Todd Zeile to fill the void. And the 2000 cast of characters didn't disappoint, winning a wild card playoff berth with a 94-victory season. Each player is listed with his uniform number, primary position, 2000 regular-season statistics while with the Mets and career statistics. Congratulations to the New York Mets, the 2000 National League champions!

For the past five seasons, Bobby Valentine has been the guiding force of the New York Mets. Valentine took over managerial duties of the Mets at the tail end of the 1996 season, and the Mets have since blossomed into a National League East powerhouse. The Mets improved by 17 games in Valentine's first full season as skipper. Prior to his tenure with the Mets, Valentine was the winningest manager in the history of the Texas Rangers, although they never made the playoffs. Valentine's postseason drought ended in 1999 when the Mets were the wild card team thanks to their 97 wins.

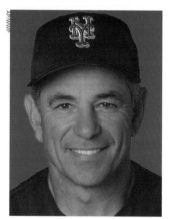

Bobby
Valentine

Manager	Wins	Losses	Pctg.	Finish
2000	94	68	.580	2nd, National League wild card
Career	960	906	.516	—

Edgardo Alfonzo 13

How good is Edgardo Alfonzo? He's so good that Yankees shortstop Derek Jeter called him his idol. One of baseball's rising stars, the Venezuelan-born Alfonzo made his major league debut in 1995 with the Mets, who signed him to a minor league contract as a free agent in 1991. The second baseman posted an impressive 1999 season, proving his mettle as one of the best all-around players in the league. That year, he racked up six hits in one game. A versatile player for the Mets, Alfonzo has played primarily as a second baseman, but has also played third base and shortstop. Alfonzo's numbers continued to improve in 2000, further cementing his status as a player to watch.

Second Base	Avg.	AB	Hits	HR	RBI
2000	.324	544	176	25	94
Career	.296	2950	874	87	433

API/WWP

API/WWP

Armando Benitez

49

Relief pitcher Armando Benitez is garnering an impressive reputation with the Mets. The former Oriole struck out 321 batters over a three-year span, a number that is second in that period only to the Astros' Billy Wagner, who had 327. In 1999, he held hitters to a .148 batting average, which was the second lowest in the major leagues. Benitez started 1999 as a setup man for John Franco, but stepped in as closer when Franco was injured in July of that year. His 14.77 strikeout average per 9 innings in 1999 set a record among major league pitchers who threw in 75 or more games. In 2000, the Mets have looked to Benitez as a closer who can get the job done, as evidenced by his 41 saves in the 2000 season. The right-hander has an impressive fastball and splitter in his arsenal.

Pitcher	W-L	ERA	Games	Saves	IP	K
2000	4-4	2.61	76	41	76.0	106
Career	19-23	3.04	360	100	367.2	517

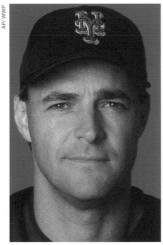

AP/ WWP

AP/ WWP

Al
Leiter
22

Al Leiter makes it look so easy. Year in year out, he puts up solid numbers that have earned him a place in Mets fans' hearts. Although he endured arthroscopic surgery on his left knee prior to the start of the 2000 season, Leiter continued to have another stellar season. His 16 wins in 2000 fell one short of his career best, while his 200 strikeouts tied his career-high set in 1996. In his three seasons as a Met, Leiter has won 46 games and fanned 536 batters. Leiter can often be counted on to go the distance for the Mets, hurling 13 complete games over the past eight seasons. As a Florida Marlin, Leiter pitched the first no-hitter in franchise history for the team in 1996 That same year, he recorded the last out for the National League in the All-Star Game.

Pitcher	W-L	ERA	Games	Saves	IP	K
2000	16-8	3.20	31	0	208.0	200
Career	106-79	3.73	264	2	1502.2	1307

AP/ WWP

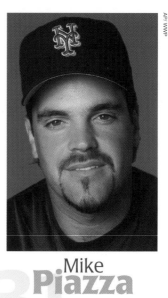

AP/ WWP

Mike
31 Piazza

An opposing team's lead is never safe as long as Mike Piazza is in the lineup for the Mets. Piazza's crushing power has become the stuff of legends over the course of his nine seasons in the majors. This eight-time All-Star belted 38 home runs in 2000, three of which were grand slams. His .324 average and 113 RBIs placed him among the leaders in the National League. Piazza began his career with the Los Angeles Dodgers, but he has quickly won over the hearts of new York Mets fans.

As long as Piazza keeps having multiple home run games, opposing pitchers will never get an easy night's sleep knowing that he awaits them in the lineup on game day.

Catcher	Avg.	AB	Hits	HR	RBI
2000	.324	482	156	38	113
Career	.328	4135	1356	278	881

Few players fly around the basepaths with more intensity than Kurt Abbott. Although he does not possess blazing speed, his heads-up style of play was responsible for three inside-the-park home runs for the Florida Marlins, two in 1995 and one in 1997. Abbott's 19 triples set a record while he was with the Marlins. After arriving in New York from the Colorado Rockies, Abbott had 34 hits in 157 at-bats for the Mets during the 2000 season.

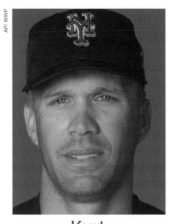

AP/ WWP

Kurt
Abbott

Shortstop	Avg.	AB	Hits	HR	RBI
2000	.217	157	34	6	12
Career	.256	2035	521	62	242

It may have appeared that Benny Agbayani came out of nowhere to blast 10 homers for the Mets in the span of 73 at-bats in 1999, but boppin' Benny from Hawaii had been biding his time in the minors since being drafted in 1993. A brief call-up in 1998 hadn't turned any heads, but Agbayani would make the most of his second chance the following season.

While Benny wasn't able to keep up his extraordinary home run pace over the course of the 2000 season, he had plenty of pop in his bat to prove that his torrid 1999 numbers were not an aberration.

AP/ WWP

Benny

Outfield	Avg.	AB	Hits	HR	RBI
2000	.289	350	101	15	60
Career	.284	641	182	29	102

Following a 1999 season that was disappointing by any yardstick, Derek Bell started the 2000 season on the Mets with a few things to prove to himself and his new team. In his fifth year in Houston, Bell had a career-high 129 strikeouts and batted an unusually low .236. But after being traded by the Astros, Bell roared back with the Mets.

Bell has always been a batter capable of offensive fireworks. He had a career-high 22 homers and a career-high 198 hits in 1998.

Derek **Bell** 16

Outfield	Avg.	AB	Hits	HR	RBI
2000	.266	546	145	18	69
Career	.279	4422	1235	129	655

Has Mike Bordick found a way to cheat Father Time? Over the past three seasons, Bordick has seen most of his offensive numbers rise each year. Filling in for injured shortstop Rey Ordonez, Bordick arrived from the Baltimore Orioles at the end of July, and proceeded to have a career year in home runs (20), runs batted in (80) and batting average (.285) over the course of the year for both teams.

Mike **Bordick** 17

Shortstop	Avg.	AB	Hits	HR	RBI
2000	.260	192	50	4	21
Career	.262	4831	1264	71	506

What's cooking with Dennis Cook? In 1999, the left-hander set a career-high with 10 wins, faded in the stretch and rebounded in the playoffs. Cook's wins were down slightly in 2000, but he kept the Mets competitive, striking out 53 batters in 59 innings.

Unlike most pitchers, Cook is never an easy out when he steps up to the plate for an at-bat. During seasons in Philadelphia and Florida, Cook was used as both a pinch runner and pinch hitter.

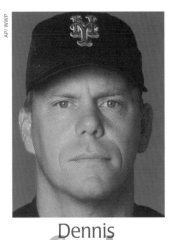

Dennis
Cook

Pitcher	W-L	ERA	Games	Saves	IP	K
2000	6-3	5.34	68	2	59.0	53
Career	62-44	3.90	566	9	942.0	688

How do you spell relief? For 17 seasons, the letters F-R-A-N-C-O have been intimidating opposing batters during the late innings of close ballgames. Franco led the league in saves in 1988 (39), 1990 (33) and 1994 (30). A five-time All-Star, Franco's 420 career saves place him behind only Lee Smith on the all-time list.

With Armando Benitez now handling much of the closer work for the Mets, Franco has adapted to become one of the most devastating setup men in the game. In just over 55 innings in 2000, Franco only allowed 46 hits and 24 runs.

John
Franco

Pitcher	W-L	ERA	Games	Saves	IP	K
2000	5-4	3.40	62	4	55.2	56
Career	82-74	2.68	940	420	1097.0	857

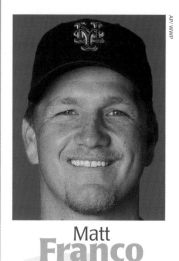

AP/ WWP

Matt
Franco
15

When the Mets need help in a pinch, they often call on Matt Franco to deliver the goods. An expert at working the count, Franco's 20 walks as a pinch hitter set a major league record in 1999. Franco can also get the big hit when needed in a clutch situation.

Franco can be counted on to play a number of positions. While in 2000 Franco spent most of his time at first base, he also played second and third base, as well in the outfield. In 1999, he was also called in to pitch an inning!

First Base	Avg.	AB	Hits	HR	RBI
2000	.239	134	32	2	14
Career	.255	638	163	13	72

AP/ WWP

Darryl
Hamilton
18

Although Darryl Hamilton can beat you with his bat, it's his glove that sends batters back to the dugout shaking their heads after he has robbed them of a hit with a stellar play in center field. Hamilton has hit over .300 four times in his career, and he has possessed a perfect 1.000 fielding percentage six times while in the big leagues. For this left-handed batter, there's no place quite like home. After coming to the Mets during the 1999 season, Hamilton hit an impressive .339 for his new team. Some pitchers would rather stay at home than face such a hot hitter!

Outfield	Avg.	A.B.	Hits	H.R.	RBI
2000	.276	105	29	1	6
Career	.293	4451	1306	50	449

If the New York Mets most closely resembled a puzzle, Mike Hampton just might represent the missing piece. Before being brought over in a deal from the Houston Astros, Hampton was the winningest pitcher in the National League in 1999 with 22 wins. He kept up his successful ways in 2000, contributing 15 wins for the Mets. His ERA of 3.14 was fourth-best in the league in 2000. This slinging southpaw has had over 100 strikeouts in each of his last six seasons, thanks in part to his wicked sinker.

Mike
Hampton

Pitcher	W-L	ERA	Games	Saves	IP	K
2000	15-10	3.14	33	0	217.2	151
Career	85-53	3.44	241	1	1260.2	852

Lenny Harris can start a game off on the right foot with a leadoff homer or finish the game off with late inning heroics. A talented journeyman who has spent time in Cincinnati, Los Angeles, Colorado and Arizona, Harris enjoyed his second stint with the Mets in 2000. Harris had previously played for New York for a brief period in 1998.

Lenny
Harris

Third Base	Avg.	AB	Hits	HR	RBI
2000	.304	138	42	3	13
Career	.273	3282	895	31	305

AP/ WWP

Bobby J.
Jones
28

Selected as a compensation pick between the first and second rounds of the 1991 free agent draft, Bobby J. Jones has played his entire Major League career with the Mets. He missed most of last season with injuries and was practically written off as a has-been at the start of this season. But when he returned from a stint with the Mets' AAA team in Norfolk, Virginia, things started coming together for the right-hander. He pitched a complete game against the Cardinals in July and went on to put together a respectable 11-6 record for the season.

Pitcher	W-L	ERA	Games	Saves	IP	K
2000	11-6	5.06	27	0	154.2	85
Career	74-56	4.13	193	0	1215.2	714

AP/ WWP

Joe
McEwing
47

"Super Joe" McEwing came over to the Mets from the Cardinals at the start of the 2000 season. He's a terrific utility player who can play nearly every defensive position. He had some ups-and-downs in his first season with the Mets, but he's not called Super Joe for nothing, and has been able to contribute in the clutch. During his three years in the majors, McEwing has exhibited his versatility by playing every position except pitcher and catcher.

Outfield	Avg.	AB	Hits	HR	RBI
2000	.222	153	34	2	19
Career	.261	686	179	11	64

Talented shortstop Rey Ordonez went out for the season with a broken arm sustained during a game in May against the Dodgers. The news came as a blow, but everyone was optimistic that he would be back in six weeks. However, upon closer examination, it was determined that Ordonez's injury would put him out for the season. Ordonez is far more respected for his fielding than for his batting – he committed just four errors in all of the 1999 season. Ordonez has also received three Gold Glove awards for his abilities.

Rey
Ordonez
10

Shortstop	Avg.	AB	Hits	HR	RBI
2000	.188	133	25	0	9
Career	.243	2016	489	4	174

In his first full season with the Mets in 2000, outfielder Jay Payton played in 149 games and put together a .291 batting average. Payton has come through in the clutch several times for the Mets, including hitting a game-winning 10th-inning home run against the Brewers in September. He whacked his first career grand slam home run toward the end of the season in a game against the Montreal Expos. Payton hails from the Buckeye State of Ohio.

Jay
Payton
44

Outfield	Avg.	AB	Hits	HR	RBI
2000	.291	488	142	17	62
Career	.292	518	151	17	63

AP/ WWP

Timo
Perez
6

Timo Perez made quite an impact on the Mets after coming up from the minor leagues in 2000. His first career home run in September was an inside-the-park shot, the Mets' first in more than five years. Perez continued to shine in the postseason, going on an incredible five-game hitting streak. In his 24 regular-season games, Perez, a native of the Dominican Republic, smacked 14 hits and went on to score a remarkable 11 runs. This rookie's play leaves all Met fans – and all of the Mets' opponents – quivering in their seats waiting to see what he will achieve next year!

Outfield	Avg.	AB	Hits	HR	RBI
2000	.286	49	14	1	3
Career	.286	49	14	1	3

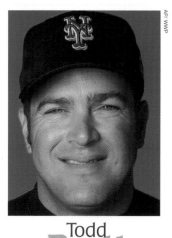

AP/ WWP

Todd
Pratt
7

As catcher Mike Piazza's back-up, Todd Pratt has some seriously large shoes to fill. Although he only played in 80 games this season, Pratt gets the job done, and does it well. Indeed, one of the areas Pratt excels in is nailing crafty runners who try to steal bases on him. The right-hander is a threat coming off the bench, as he proved in a game against the Dodgers this year. He crushed a pinch-hit grand-slam home run to contribute to the Mets' dramatic come-from-behind victory. A versatile player, Pratt can also play first base or the outfield when called upon.

Catcher	Avg.	AB	Hits	HR	RBI
2000	.275	160	44	8	25
Career	.260	770	200	24	119

The 2000 season had a familiar feel for starting pitcher Rick Reed – he posted the same won-loss record in 2000 as he did in 1999. Reed overcame a tough injury this year, getting his non-throwing hand smashed by a line drive off the bat of Marquis Grissom of the Brewers. He came back from the injury and went on to post an admirable 11-5 record. Reed, a 12-year big-league veteran, is generous with his salary: he contributes $2,000 to the American Diabetes Association for each win he accumulates.

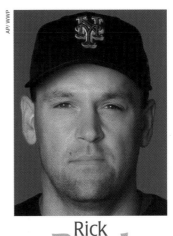

Rick
Reed
35

Pitcher	W-L	ERA	Games	Saves	IP	K
2000	11-5	4.11	30	0	184.0	121
Career	60-45	3.93	181	1	1,020.1	636

Glendon Rusch had a very good year in his first full season with the Mets and fourth professional season. He had a 12-25 career record before coming over from the Kansas City Royals and found success in his new Shea Stadium home. He lowered his ERA by one full run over his career statistics and racked up an amazing 157-44 strikeout-to-walk ratio. Rusch had a career-high in strikeouts against the Yankees in July, when he pitched a complete game and struck out 10. His previous best single-game strikeout performance was seven.

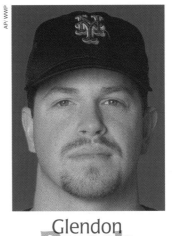

Glendon
Rusch
48

Pitcher	W-L	ERA	Games	Saves	IP	K
2000	11-11	4.01	31	0	190.2	157
Career	23-36	5.13	94	1	520.2	371

AP/WWP

Outfielder Bubba Trammell came to the Mets from the Tampa Bay Devil Rays mid-way through the 2000 season. His impact was immediate, as he bashed a three-run home run in his first at-bat. Trammell's role with the Mets is as a utility outfielder and a right-handed bat off of the bench.

Bubba
Trammell
33

Outfield	Avg.	AB	Hits	HR	RBI
2000	.232	56	13	3	12
Career	.273	850	232	40	132

AP/WWP

Robin Ventura came over to the National League and the Mets in 1999 after playing 10 seasons – his entire career – with the Chicago White Sox. Ventura made an easy transition, hitting .301 and ringing up 120 RBI in his first year in the NL. His defense was solid as well, and Ventura earned a Gold Glove – his sixth! Ventura had shoulder surgery prior to this season and it might have affected his game, as the numbers he posted in 2000 weren't as good as what he's proven capable of. The Mets remained true to him, however, and he played in nearly every game.

Robin
Ventura
4

Third Base	Avg.	AB	Hits	HR	RBI
2000	.232	469	109	24	84
Career	.273	5599	1530	227	945

During the 2000 regular season, Turk Wendell pitched in 77 games, and struck out 73 batters in 82.2 innings. A quirky, eight-year veteran of the major leagues, he has played for only two teams, the Chicago Cubs and the New York Mets. Playing for the Mets since 1998, Wendell is feared for his slider, a pitch that has taken many forms coming from Wendell's hand.

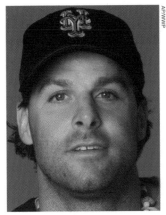

Turk
Wendell
99

Pitcher	W-L	ERA	Games	Saves	IP	K
2000	8-6	3.59	77	1	82.2	73
Career	29-25	3.83	414	31	498.0	421

Starting his major league career with the Pittsburgh Pirates in 1994, Rick White was sidelined during 1996 due to elbow surgery. Signed by the Tampa Bay Devil Rays in 1997, White spent a year at their affiliate in Orlando and then returned to major league play in 1998. He had an impressive 1999 season and set a career-high with 63 appearances. White was acquired by the Mets in July to serve as a relief pitcher.

Rick
White
51

Pitcher	W-L	ERA	Games	Saves	IP	K
2000	2-3	3.81	22	1	28.1	67
Career	18-26	3.94	225	9	406.2	254

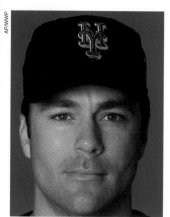

AP/WWP

Veteran Todd Zeile began his career in 1989 with St. Louis and played, primarily as a third baseman, with the Cubs, Phillies, Orioles, Dodgers and Marlins before joining the Texas Rangers in 1998. Zeile signed a three-year deal with the Mets before the 2000 season, and looked to help fill the gap at first base left by John Olerud. Zeile played in 153 games this season and reached a career benchmark, swatting his 200th home run.

Todd Zeile
9

First Base	Avg.	AB	Hits	HR	RBI
2000	.268	544	146	22	79
Career	.268	5889	1576	205	884

Other Mets Players

Other players made contributions to the Mets during the course of the 2000 regular season. Here's a look at a few Mets:

After his debut in 1992 with the Minnesota Twins, relief pitcher Pat Mahomes was traded to the Boston Red Sox in 1996, only to join the Mets in 1999. Pitcher Bobby M. Jones (not to be confused with another Mets pitcher Bobby *J.* Jones) joined the Mets in 2000 from the Colorado Rockies. A left-handed thrower, Jones is known for a low-90s fastball and a hard-breaking slider which is particularly effective in striking out right-handed batters. Holding positions on both first base and in left field, #30 Jorge Toca made his major league debut with the Mets in 1999.

New York Mets pitching coach, Al Jackson, is no stranger to baseball or the Mets. Born in 1935, Jackson began his career as a pitcher with the Pittsburgh Pirates in 1959. Jackson remained with the Pirates for only two years, leaving the team to join the Mets for their 1962 inaugural season. Jackson retired in 1969, but not before moving to the St. Louis Cardinals, rejoining the Mets and playing for the Cincinnati Reds. A southpaw, Jackson was credited with a 3.98 ERA in his 1389.1 innings pitched.

Al
Jackson
54
Bullpen Coach

* Picture features Jackson in his playing days

Former first baseman Tom Robson has been a major league coach for 11 years, four of them with the Mets. He was part of manager Bobby Valentine's staff with the Texas Rangers from 1986 to 1992, and then spent two seasons as hitting coach of the Chiba Lotte Marines of the Japanese Pacific League. In June 1999, the Mets fired Robson and two other coaches during the team's longest losing streak since 1996. Robson was rehired in October 1999.

Tom
Robson
53
Hitting Coach

Born in Havana, Cuba in 1939, Octavio Victor "Cookie" Rojas enjoyed a 16-year career in the big leagues with Cincinnati, Philadelphia, St. Louis and Kansas City. A five-time All Star with 1660 career hits, Rojas' first bench job came as manager of the California Angels in 1988. He joined the Mets as third base coach in 1997.

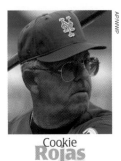

Cookie
Rojas
8
Third Base Coach

John
Stearns
12
Catching Coach

Longtime Mets catcher John Stearns played all but one at-bat of his 11-year career(1974-1984) with the Mets. He achieved All-Star status in 1977, 1979, 1980 and 1982. Stearns coached for the Baltimore Orioles before becoming the Mets' catching coach in 2000.

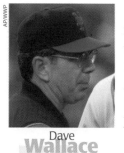

Dave
Wallace
52
Pitching Coach

Born on September 9, 1947, David Wallace made his major league pitching debut in 1973 with the Philadelphia Phillies. After spending the early 1970s as a relief pitcher, Wallace left the Phillies and went north to pitch for the Toronto Blue Jays in 1978. Wallace was named pitching coach for the Mets on June 5, 1999, replacing Bob Apodaca.

Mookie
Wilson
1
First Base Coach

Mookie Wilson has a special place reserved in Mets' history. He's best known for bringing the tying run home by dodging a wild pitch during the 10th inning of the 1986 World Series. That same at-bat, he hit the would-be single that slipped through Bill Buckner's legs allowing Ray Knight to score the run that won the series for the Mets. Wilson was traded to Toronto in 1989, ending his 10-season playing career with the Mets. Today, he's the first base coach for the Mets.

Let's Go Mets!
– An Amazin' History

1960s

From Worst To First

In the wake of the departure of the Giants and Dodgers in the late 1950s, the mayor of New York City set up a committee to lure an established National League team to the city. Lawyer William Shea spearheaded the effort and courted the Phillies, Reds and Pirates, to no avail. Finally, he teamed up with Branch Rickey to form a rival league, the Continental League. Faced with the prospect of unwanted competition, Major League Baseball "rewarded" Shea's efforts with one of two new expansion teams in 1962 – and the National League's New York Metropolitans were born!

AP/WWP

Manager Casey Stengel during the Mets' inaugural season.

The Mets played at the Polo Grounds and were managed by Casey Stengel, a New York baseball legend whose strange style fit the Mets perfectly. Built on a patchwork roster of cast-offs and rookies including Choo Choo Coleman, "Marvelous" Marv Throneberry and Don Zimmer, the Mets were inept from the start. The team lost a record 120 games, and finished dead last in every statistical category.

But these losers were a lovable lot and their futility only endeared them to a growing core of fans, many of whom were former Giants and Dodgers fans. The Mets' new ballpark in Queens, Shea

Year-By-Year Records			
YEAR	PLACE	RECORD	PCTG.
1962	10th	40-120	.250
1963	10th	51-111	.315
1964	10th	53-109	.327
1965	10th	50-112	.309
1966	9th	66-95	.410
1967	10th	61-101	.377
1968	9th	73-89	.451
1969	1st	100-62	.617
Total		494-799	.382

Red denotes World Series title

Stadium, opened in 1964. For the first decade of their existence, the "Amazin' Mets" were a team you could root for with a clear conscience – if you could stand to watch them play!

By the late 1960s, Mets fans had reason to hope, despite being the league's perennial bottom feeder. But acquisitions like relief ace Tug McGraw, speedy center fielder Tommie Agee and future Hall-of-Famers Tom Seaver (1967 Rookie of the Year) and Nolan Ryan helped the Mets to 73 wins in 1968.

Nolan Ryan pitched for the Mets from 1966 to 1971.

The team was getting better – but no one could have predicted the wild ride the Mets would take in 1969! The Mets put together a September winning streak that shot them past the floundering Chicago Cubs. By season's end, the Mets had a shocking 100 wins and landed their first postseason berth by eight games. Great individual seasons by Cy Young Award winner Seaver (25 wins), Agee (26 HR) and Cleon Jones (.340) put the Mets on top. The "Miracle Mets" then swept Hank Aaron's Atlanta Braves in the N.L.C.S. to land in the club's first World Series.

The New York Mets celebrate their World Series title in 1969.

On paper, the Mets couldn't match the powerhouse AL champion Baltimore Orioles, who had great hitters (Frank Robinson, Boog Powell), great pitchers (Mike Cuellar, Jim Palmer) and great glove men (Brooks Robinson, Mark Belanger). Most people expected the Orioles to clobber the Mets and Baltimore took Game 1 by a 4-1 score. The Mets gutted out a 2-1 win in Game 2, while Tommie Agee single-handedly gave Game 3 to the Mets by making two game-saving catches.

Not to be outdone, right fielder Ron Swoboda cut down an Orioles rally with a diving catch to preserve Game 4 for the Mets. The Orioles went up early in Game 5, but the Mets roared back to win 5-3, and the Shea Stadium fans went nuts! After seven years of futility, the Mets closed the 1960s on top of the world!

World Series History

YEAR OPPONENT	RESULT
1969 Baltimore Orioles	W, 4-1

1970s

Diamonds In The Rough

After ending the 1960s on a great high, the Mets spent the early 1970s locked in third place with 83 wins for three consecutive years.

AP/WWP

They battled hard (especially in 1970, losing the division to Pittsburgh on September 27), but a slew of injuries kept the Mets floundering. After the 1971 season, the club traded fireballer Nolan Ryan to the California Angels for shortstop Jim Fregosi – a move that, in hindsight, was probably one of the worst trades in Mets history.

Mets pitcher Tom Seaver had some dominating seasons in the 1970s.

Perhaps the biggest bright spot of the early part of the decade came on April 22, 1970, when Tom Seaver struck out 19 Padres en route to a season that saw the righthander throw 21 complete games and post a ridiculously low 1.76 ERA.

The Mets battled to win the NL East title in 1973, thanks to the efforts of Cy Young winner Seaver (19-10, 2.08), John Milner (23 HRs, club-leading 72 RBI) and George Stone (12-3). After taking out Pete Rose and the Cincinnati Reds in the N.L.C.S., the Mets fought bravely but lost to the powerful Oakland A's in the World Series.

Year-By-Year Records			
YEAR	PLACE	RECORD	PCTG.
1970	3rd	83-79	.512
1971	T-3rd	83-79	.512
1972	3rd	83-73	.532
1973	1st	82-79	.509
1974	5th	71-91	.438
1975	T-3rd	82-80	.506
1976	3rd	86-76	.531
1977	6th	64-98	.395
1978	6th	66-96	.407
1979	6th	63-99	.389
Total		763-850	.473

The rest of the decade was a tale of mediocrity and worse, featuring revolving door rosters and the shocking trade of Tom Seaver to the Reds in 1977. In 1979, the Mets lost 99 games and finished 35 games out of first, while Seaver's Reds won the West Division.

World Series History	
YEAR OPPONENT	RESULT
1973 Oakland A's	L, 3-4

119

1980s

The Doctor Is In

The Mets opened the decade the way they ended the 1970s. Had it not been for the player's strike in 1981, the Mets would have lost at least 94 games for seven years in a row! Still, the Mets' home attendance was on the rise and some players turned in great individual efforts, including Dave Kingman, Neil Allen, Jesse Orosco and Tom Seaver, who returned for the 1983 season and threw six shutout innings on Opening Day.

Two great Mets pitchers, Tom Seaver and Dwight Gooden.

By the mid-1980s, some key personnel moves put the Mets on the winning track. The club brought in Gold Glove first baseman Keith Hernandez, hard-nosed catcher Gary Carter and veteran third baseman Ray Knight via trade and brought slugger Darryl Strawberry and pitcher Ron Darling up from the farm system. Under new manager Davey Johnson, the Mets reversed their fortunes and finished in second place in 1984 and 1985.

But no one made a more explosive impact than Dwight "Doc" Gooden. Voted Rookie of the Year in 1984 for his 276 strikeouts (a rookie record), Gooden continued to throw laser beams on his way to winning the pitching triple crown in 1985 (24-4, 268 strikeouts, 1.53 ERA).

The Mets were the class of baseball in 1986, winning 108 games and winning the NL East title, largely due to the pitching rotation of Gooden (17-6), Darling

Year-By-Year Records

YEAR	PLACE	RECORD	PCTG.
1980	5th	67-95	.414
1981	5th	41-62	.398
1982	6th	65-97	.401
1983	6th	68-94	.420
1984	2nd	90-72	.556
1985	2nd	98-64	.605
1986	1st	108-54	.667
1987	2nd	92-70	.568
1988	1st	100-60	.625
1989	2nd	87-75	.537
Total		816-743	.519

Red denotes World Series title

(15-6), Bob Ojeda (18-5) and Sid Fernandez (16-6). The Mets grueling N.L.C.S. battle against the Houston Astros will be remembered for Dykstra's clutch ninth inning homer to win Game 5, and the Game 6

AP/WWP

marathon in which the Mets outscored Houston 3-2 in the 16th inning to win the series.

The 1986 World Series saw the Mets fall behind the Boston Red Sox (led by Cy Young winner Roger Clemens and batting champion Wade Boggs) three games to two setting up the unforgettable finish in pivotal Game 6.

Mookie Wilson slides back into first safely as Game 6 goat Bill Buckner applies the tag in 1986.

Trailing 5-3 with two out in the 10th inning, the Mets tied the game on three singles and a wild pitch. With the winning run at third, Mookie Wilson hit a routine bouncer to first base. In a now-classic World Series moment, the ball skidded right under Bill Buckner's glove and Ray Knight danced home with the winning run for a miraculous Game 6 victory! The Mets went on to win the series with an 8-5 victory in Game 7, capping off one of the greatest seasons in baseball history with the franchise's second world championship and first in 17 seasons.

AP/WWP

1986 World Series MVP Ray Knight celebrates the Mets' championship with catcher Gary Carter.

The Mets returned to the postseason in 1988, winning 100 games behind Strawberry's 39 home runs, Randy Myers' 26 saves and David Cone's 20-3, 2.22 ERA season. Although they played well in the N.L.C.S., the Mets fell to Orel Hershiser, Kirk Gibson and the Dodgers in seven games.

World Series History

YEAR	OPPONENT	RESULT
1986	Boston Red Sox	W, 4-3

1990s

So Close, Yet So Far Away

The 1990 edition of the Mets won 91 games and finished in second place, the final year of an amazing seven-year run of finishing in either first or second place. Some of the new faces doing the job for New York included longtime Minnesota Twin Frank Viola (20 wins), former Cincinnati pitcher John Franco (NL-leading 33 saves) and third baseman Dave Magadan (.328).

AP/WWP

Mets fans were treated to several individual feats in the 1991. Howard Johnson led the league in homers with 38, and became a three-time member of the 30-30 club. And David Cone created excitement by striking out 19 Phillies in the last game of the season and leading the league in strikeouts for the second straight year.

Reliever John Franco, one of the Mets' best pitchers in the 1990s.

But injuries and age finally took their toll. By 1993, the team was in seventh place, had one of its weakest lineups in years, and suffered bad luck at every turn. Just ask Anthony Young, the righthander who set a record with 27 straight losses between 1992-1993.

While the 1994 club won't be remembered for the biggest names in history with steady but unspectacular players like Fernando Vina, Rico Brogna and Jose Vizcaino, the team's third-place finish brought the New York Mets back to respectability.

Over the next three years, the Mets retooled with a mix of young pitchers (Jason Isringhausen, Bill Pulsipher) and

Year-By-Year Records

YEAR	PLACE	RECORD	PCTG.
1990	2nd	91-71	.562
1991	5th	77-84	.478
1992	5th	72-90	.444
1993	7th	59-103	.364
1994	3rd	55-58	.487
1995	T-2nd	69-75	.479
1996	4th	71-91	.438
1997	3rd	88-74	.543
1998	2nd	88-74	.543
1999	2nd	97-66	.595
Total		767-786	.492

veteran hitters (Bernard Gilkey, Lance Johnson), and added some pop in the form of second-generation major leaguer, catcher Todd Hundley (41 HRs in 1996).

By 1998, first baseman John Olerud, pitchers Al Leiter and Rick Reed and acrobatic shortstop Rey Ordonez gave the Mets a solid core that carried the team to back-to-back 88-win seasons. But the Mets

really charged into the limelight with the mid-year acquisition of catcher Mike Piazza, who put up great numbers (.330 average, 32 HR, 111 RBI) despite playing for three teams.

The Mets finished second in 1999 and set off on a crazy play-off ride by catching the Reds in the wild card race on the final

Mike Piazza's devastating home run stroke.

weekend and winning a one-game playoff, 5-0. After taking care of the Arizona Diamondbacks in the divisional series, the Mets ran into their perennial rivals, the Atlanta Braves, in the National League Championship Series.

In one of the wildest series ever, the Mets lost the first three games before winning Game 4. Game 5 was an extra-inning affair. The 15th inning began with the teams tied at 2, but the Braves scored a run in the top of the inning. Faced with elimination, the Mets won the game on Robin Ventura's dramatic grand slam, later changed officially to a single because the jubilant Ventura never reached second base.

The Mets celebrate Robin Ventura's game-winning hit in Game 5 of the 1999 N.L.C.S.

But the Mets went down in Game 6, losing on a bases-loaded walk by Mets pitcher Kenny Rogers and ending an amazing postseason run.

Subway Series Memorabilia 2000

Subway Series matchups don't roll down the tracks every year. In fact, before the 2000 event, there hadn't been a Subway Series since 1956, when the Yankees faced off against the Brooklyn Dodgers. So you better believe that the World Series 2000 between the Yankees and the Mets is one that fans are going to want to remember forever.

The following section spotlights some of the new Subway Series memorabilia that is sure be a hit with both Yankees and Mets fans – and baseball fans in general. The products range from programs and tickets stubs to T-shirts and baseball caps. Each item is listed with a description, manufacturer's name and retail price range if applicable (prices subject to change, "N/A" means the price was unavailable at time of printing). And this is just the pre-game show! Keep your eyes out for more post-series memorabilia, including cards from Upper Deck and Topps.

Collecting baseball memorabilia is one of America's most popular pastimes. Great baseball artifacts from days long ago can often only be found in the Baseball Hall of Fame or in your grandfather's attic (if you're lucky). Why is collecting so popular? Probably because it's something that will help fans retain their memories of that special game, season or player. And quite often, the memorabilia will be valuable, if not monetarily, then at least sentimentally.

Right now, the new Subway Series products are available in retail outlets, but once the series is over, they are sure to become collector's items. See the sections on *Subway Series Memorabilia 1921-1956* and *New York Baseball Memorabilia 1903-Present Day* later in the book for a look at how some other baseball memorabilia has increased in value.

Programs

The official World Series program is a grand slam of information for every fan. With replays such as "2000: The Year in Review" and "2000 World Series Participants" and hits such as "Debate at the Plate" (the presidential candidates talk baseball), this $10 purchase is sure to score. The program can be found in stores, as well as Major League Baseball's store at *www.mlb.com* or 1-800-704-2937.

Cover

Inside Pages

World Series 2000 Fall Classic® Major League Baseball® Official Program
Retail Price: $10.00

Tickets & Ticket Stubs

Tickets that get you through the stadium gate are truly coveted (because it means you're going to the game!), but ticket stubs have their value as well so make sure you save them. Here is a glimpse at some of the tickets that got some very lucky fans into the 2000 World Series games.

Game 1
Yankees Stadium

Game 2
Yankees Stadium

Game 3
Shea Stadium

Game 4
Shea Stadium

Publications

The World Series is already big news, but the first Subway Series in over 44 years makes even bigger headlines. In a time of political debates and international unrest, baseball is still front-cover news that is fit to print. In addition to newspapers, there will be magazines that will have special Subway Series editions. Here's a look at how some New York newspapers chronicled the story.

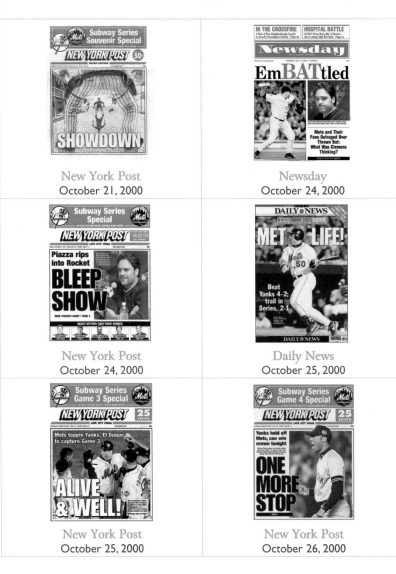

New York Post
October 21, 2000

Newsday
October 24, 2000

New York Post
October 24, 2000

Daily News
October 25, 2000

New York Post
October 25, 2000

New York Post
October 26, 2000

Other Subway Series Items

The following section spotlights the wide array of products you can buy to build your own Subway Series Hall of Fame. Caps, jackets and shirts are listed first, followed by a variety of other items listed alphabetically by category (i.e. banners, baseballs, etc.). Each piece is listed with its retail price range and manufacturer.

Team Symbols And Landmarks
Retail Price: $18-20
New Era

Team Symbols Subway Series
Retail Price: $18-20
Twins Enterprise Inc.

World Series Logo
Retail Price: $19-21
Puma

World Series Jacket
Retail Price: N/A
Majestic Athletic

Blue And Orange Skyline
Retail Price: $15-17
Majestic Athletic

Jeter/Piazza Rivalry
Retail Price: $17-19
Majestic Athletic

NY vs. NY
Retail Price: N/A
Nike

The Real Fall Classic
Retail Price: N/A
Nike

Roster (long sleeve)
Retail Price: N/A
Puma

Series Rumble
Retail Price: $17-20
Lee Sport

Artist Rendering

Subway Series Jersey
Retail Price: $40-45
Majestic Athletic

Subway Series Sweatshirt
Retail Price: $30-35
Lee Sport

Artist Rendering

Subway Series Tee (toddler)
Retail Price: $10-12
Lee Sport

Subway Train (black)
Retail Price: $17-20
Majestic Athletic

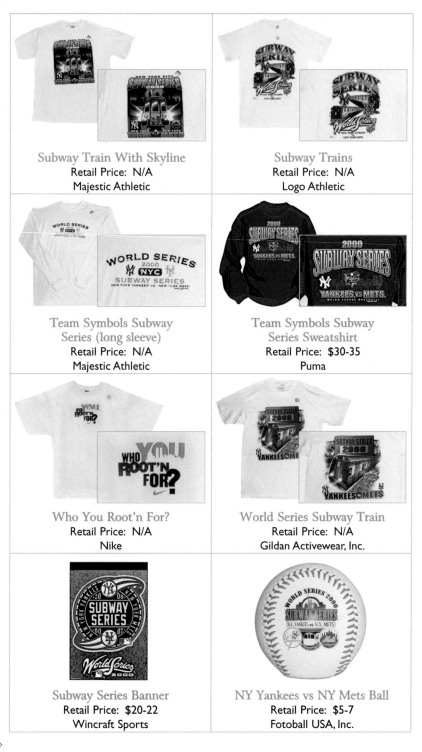

Subway Train With Skyline
Retail Price: N/A
Majestic Athletic

Subway Trains
Retail Price: N/A
Logo Athletic

Team Symbols Subway
Series (long sleeve)
Retail Price: N/A
Majestic Athletic

Team Symbols Subway
Series Sweatshirt
Retail Price: $30-35
Puma

Who You Root'n For?
Retail Price: N/A
Nike

World Series Subway Train
Retail Price: N/A
Gildan Activewear, Inc.

Subway Series Banner
Retail Price: $20-22
Wincraft Sports

NY Yankees vs NY Mets Ball
Retail Price: $5-7
Fotoball USA, Inc.

Official 2000 World Series Ball
Retail Price: $13-15
Rawlings Sporting Goods

Official 2000 World Series Ball
With Display Case
Retail Price: $65-70
Caseworks International, Inc.

*Artist Rendering,
Shows Flaps*

Subway Series World Series Ball
Retail Price: $25-30
Rawlings Sporting Goods

Subway Series 2000
Engraved Display Case
Retail Price: $28-30
Caseworks International, Inc.

Subway Series 2000 Engraved
Tall Display Case
Retail Price: $45-50
Caseworks International, Inc.

World Series 2000 Logo Emblem
Retail Price: $10-12
National Emblem

Subway Series Flag
Retail Price: $15-17
Rico Tag Express

Back

Front

Token Bronze Medallion
Retail Price: $20-22
Steiner Sports

Token Silver Medallion
Retail Price: $40-42
Steiner Sports

Back

Front

Welcome To The
Subway Series Mug
Retail Price: $12-14
Hunter

Pledge Your Allegiance Pennant
Retail Price: $5-7
Wincraft Sports

Subway Series Pennant
Retail Price: $4-6
Rico Tag Express

Match Up Composite
Retail Price: $10-12
Photo File, Inc.

Dual Team Plaque
Retail Price: $60-65
Mounted Memories

Battle For The Apple Poster
Retail Price: $6-8
STARLINE INC.

Pledge Your Allegiance Poster
Retail Price: N/A
New York City Transit

**Bernie Williams Subway
Series Portrait**
Retail Price: $10-12
Photo File, Inc.

**Derek Jeter Subway
Series Portrait**
Retail Price: $10-12
Photo File, Inc.

**Edgardo Alfonzo Subway
Series Portrait**
Retail Price: $10-12
Photo File, Inc.

**Mike Piazza Subway
Series Portrait**
Retail Price: $10-12
Photo File, Inc.

Subway Series Shotglass
Retail Price: $5-7
Hunter

Official World Series Video
Retail Price: $20-22
MLB Home Video

Yankees Memorabilia 2000

How can you tell true Yankees fans? By their pinstripes of course! This section will showcase some examples of the 2000 official Yankee merchandise, along with a description, manufacturer and retail price range if applicable. So you can run out during the 7th inning stretch and pick up some things or do your shopping on-line at *www.yankees.com* or *www.majorleaguebaseball.com*.

Division Championship
Retail Price: $18-20
Puma

Gray Symbol Cap
Retail Price: $25-28
New Era

Japanese Cap
Retail Price: $30-33
N/A

Khaki Symbol Cap
Retail Price: $15-17
Twins Enterprise Inc.

Mesh Symbol Cap
Retail Price: $22-25
New Era

New York Cap
Retail Price: N/A
Nike

Red Symbol Cap
Retail Price: $30-33
New Era

Symbol Cap
Retail Price: N/A
New Era

Symbol Cap (fitted)
Retail Price: N/A
New Era

Symbol Knit Cap
Retail Price: $10-12
American Needle

White With Red And
Blue Symbol Cap
Retail Price: $25-28
New Era

World Series Cap With NY Symbol
Retail Price: N/A
Puma

Gamer Jacket
Retail Price: $90-100
Majestic Athletic

Yankees Script On Blue Jacket
Retail Price: $100-110
Majestic Athletic

Yankees Script On White Jacket
Retail Price: $100-110
Majestic Athletic

Yankees Symbol On Hooded Jacket
Retail Price: $50-55
Mighty Mac Sports

American Pastime League Champion Shirt
Retail Value: $40-45
Lee Sport

Batting Practice Jersey
Retail Value: $50-55
Majestic Athletic

Batting Practice Tee
Retail Price: $15-17
Majestic Athletic

Classic Jersey
Retail Price: $23-25
Russell Athletic

Headliner League Champion Tee
Retail Price: $17-20
Lee Sport

Home Jersey
Retail Price: $60-65
Russell Athletic

Official Clubhouse League
Championship (kids)
Retail Price: $18-20
Lee Sport

Road Jersey
Retail Price: $75-85
Majestic Athletic

Back   Front

Ruth Jersey
Retail Price: $65-70
Majestic Athletic

"Stitch In Time" League
Championship Tee
Retail Price: $17-20
Puma

Symbol 2000 Playoffs Authentic
Collection Sweatshirt
Retail Price: $40-45
Majestic Athletic

Symbol Tee
Retail Price: $15-17
Majestic Athletic

Symbol/Worn Look Tee
Retail Price: N/A
Majestic Athletic

Tour 2 Polo
Retail Price: $50-55
Antigua

Yankees Tee (long sleeve)
Retail Price: $20-22
Majestic Athletic

Yankees With Symbol
Retail Price: $15-17
Majestic Athletic

Baseball Alarm Clock
Retail Price: $32-35
N/A

Batting Hat Lamp
Retail Price: $43-48
N/A

Derek Jeter Bear
Retail Price: N/A
Salvino's Team Set 2000 Bammer

Logo Money Clip
Retail Price: $10-12
N/A

Logo Vinyl Baseball
Retail Price: $4-6
Good Stuff Corp.

NY Yankee Barbie® Doll
Retail Price: $60-65
N/A

Official 2000 New York
Team Yearbook
Retail Price: $10
N/A

Resin Santa With Symbol
Retail Price: $45-50
The Memory Company

Symbol Ornament
Retail Price: N/A
Topperscot Inc.

Symbol Pillow
Retail Price: N/A
N/A

Trading Card (Pettitte)
Retail Price: N/A
Fleer

Yankees Checkers
Retail Price: $20-22
Big League Promotions

Yankees License Plate Frame
Retail Price: $10-12
N/A

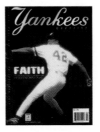

Yankees Magazine
Retail Price: $4.95
N/A

Mets Memorabilia 2000

    With everything from shirts to shorts to bobbing-head dolls, Mets fans can fill their lives with met...ropolitan style. This section will showcase some examples of the 2000 official Mets merchandise, along with manufacturer and retail price range. So head down to your local sports store or shop on-line at *www.mets.com* or *www.majorleaguebaseball.com*.

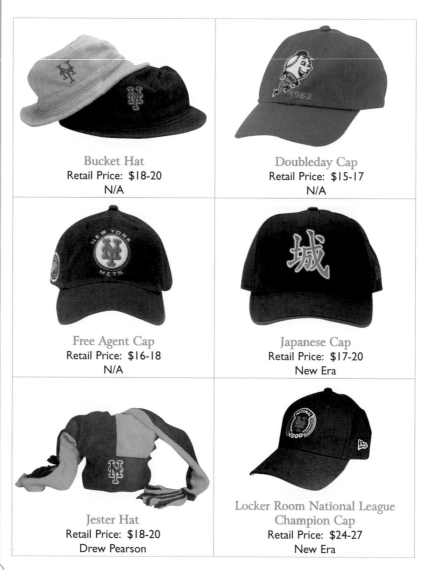

Bucket Hat
Retail Price: $18-20
N/A

Doubleday Cap
Retail Price: $15-17
N/A

Free Agent Cap
Retail Price: $16-18
N/A

Japanese Cap
Retail Price: $17-20
New Era

Jester Hat
Retail Price: $18-20
Drew Pearson

Locker Room National League Champion Cap
Retail Price: $24-27
New Era

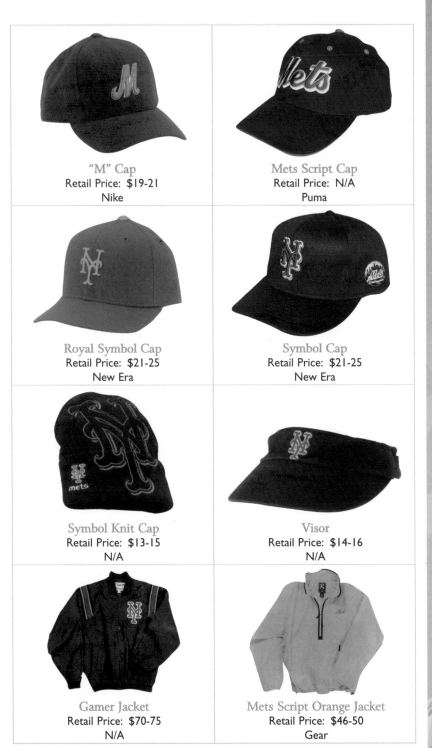

"M" Cap
Retail Price: $19-21
Nike

Mets Script Cap
Retail Price: N/A
Puma

Royal Symbol Cap
Retail Price: $21-25
New Era

Symbol Cap
Retail Price: $21-25
New Era

Symbol Knit Cap
Retail Price: $13-15
N/A

Visor
Retail Price: $14-16
N/A

Gamer Jacket
Retail Price: $70-75
N/A

Mets Script Orange Jacket
Retail Price: $46-50
Gear

Symbol Jacket
Retail Price: N/A
Majestic Athletic

1969 World Series
Retail Price: $26-30
Cooperstown Collection

Ballpark Scenes
Retail Price: $73-80
Reyn Spooner

Classic Jersey
Retail Price: $20-22
N/A

Grey Away Jersey
Retail Price: $125-135
Rawlings

Logo Vest
Retail Price: $60-65
Gear For Sports

Mesh Symbol Jersey
Retail Price: $50-55
Majestic Athletic

Mets Characters
Retail Price: $26-30
Cooperstown Collection

Mets Script Jersey
Retail Price: $70-72
Majestic Athletic

Mets Script Tee
Retail Price: $18-20
Lee Sports

Mets vs. Cardinals Championship
Retail Price: $17-20
N/A

New York Sweatshirt
Retail Price: $55-60
Gear

Official Clubhouse National League
Championship Tee
Retail Price: $20-22
Lee Sport

Official Clubhouse National League
Championship Sweatshirt
Retail Price: $30-33
Lee Sport

Opening Day In Japan
Retail Price: $19-21
N/A

Sleeveless Symbol Tee
Retail Price: $15-17
Pro Player

Symbol Sweatshirt
Retail Price: $40-45
Majestic Athletic

Logo Shorts
Retail Price: $57-60
Cutter & Buck

2000 New York Mets Yearbook
Retail Price: $10.00
N/A

Baby Bottle
Retail Price: $6-8
änsa KIDS

Beach Towel
Retail Price: $20-22
N/A

Beverage Opener Key Chain
Retail Price: $6-8
N/A

Bobbing Head Doll
Retail Price: $15-17
N/A

Cheerleader Bear
Retail Price: $31-35
Roxbury

Logo Golf Ball Caddy
Retail Price: $8-10
N/A

Logo Ornament
Retail Price: $7-9
Topperscot Inc.

Logo Shotglass
Retail Price: $4-6
Hunter

Piazza Mug
Retail Price: $10-12
Hunter

Symbol Bat
Retail Price: N/A
Coopersburg Sports

"Songs and Sounds That
Shake Shea" CD
Retail Price: $15-17
EMI

2000 Stamped Team Autographed
Baseball & Ballholder
Retail Price: $10-12
N/A

Trading Card (Ventura)
Retail Price: N/A
Fleer

Subway Series Memorabilia 1921 – 1956

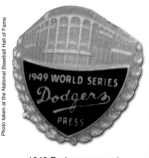

Photo taken at the National Baseball Hall of Fame

1949 Dodgers press pin

In the world of baseball collectibles and sports memorabilia, mementos from any of New York's previous World Series games are a special breed. Subway Series memorabilia consists of unique items that help make fans and collectors feel they are a part of some of the greatest games New York has ever seen. Baseball is a sport of great memories, and New York's Subway Series has provided some of the best.

While World Series memorabilia is coveted for its historical appeal, there's no denying its significant value. Some items, such as trading cards and World Series tickets, are within reach for most collectors and sports fans; other gems, such as a Giants program from 1921, may prove not only hard to find, but a little pricey as well.

Photo taken at the National Baseball Hall of Fame

1936 Giants press pin

Adding to the appeal of sports memorabilia is the thrill of finding rare, one-of-a-kind items that no one else has. Some examples of these types of elusive pieces of baseball history are Mickey Mantle's road jersey from 1956 signed by "The Mick" himself, or Joe DiMaggio's 1951 World Series ring, both of which have sold at auction for thousands of dollars. This section features a sampling of classic Subway Series memorabilia and their values. Please note that the values listed here are for the appraised values at the time of auction, not what the items sold

1955 Dodgers World Series ticket

for or their current values. After all, for many New York baseball fans, these items are truly priceless!

Programs

Programs from the early Subway Series can fetch anywhere from $100 to $4,000, and the series winner does not always command the higher value.

1941 Yankees vs. Dodgers
World Series program

	Values
❑ 1921 Giants (winner)	$1,800 – $3,500
❑ 1921 Yankees	$1,500 – $3,500
❑ 1922 Giants (winner)	$1,500 – $3,000
❑ 1922 Yankees	$1,200 – $2,750
❑ 1923 Giants	$1,200 – $3,500
❑ 1923 Yankees (winner)	$1,500 – $4,200
❑ 1936 Giants	$325 – $425
❑ 1936 Yankees (winner)	$325 – $525
❑ 1937 Giants	$300 – $425
❑ 1937 Yankees (winner)	$300 – $525
❑ 1941 Dodgers	$300 – $500
❑ 1941 Yankees (winner)	$250 – $325
❑ 1947 Dodgers	$250 – $375
❑ 1947 Yankees (winner)	$200 – $275
❑ 1949 Dodgers	$225 – $300
❑ 1949 Yankees (winner)	$200 – $250
❑ 1951 Giants	$150 – $200
❑ 1951 Yankees (winner)	$150 – $225
❑ 1952 Dodgers	$200 – $300
❑ 1952 Yankees (winner)	$150 – $200
❑ 1953 Dodgers	$175 – $325
❑ 1953 Yankees (winner)	$100 – $200
❑ 1955 Dodgers (winner)	$225 – $350
❑ 1955 Yankees	$125 – $200
❑ 1956 Dodgers	$175 – $325
❑ 1956 Yankees (winner)	$100 – $200

1955 Dodgers vs.
Yankees World Series program

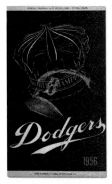

1956 Dodgers vs.
Yankees World Series program

Pennants

Nothing says "baseball" like a team pennant, especially these rare Subway Series mementos. Made of felt, pennants are hard to find in good condition due to the deterioration of their fabric. A price of $500 would be a real value, given what some of these pieces have sold for at auction.

1952 Dodgers
phantom pennant

	Values
❑ 1921 Yankees (purple & white)	$1,500 – $2,000
❑ 1923 Yankees & Giants (set/2, one each)	$1,000 – $2,000
❑ 1955 Dodgers	$500 – $700
❑ 1955 Dodgers (w/gold tassels)	$3,000 – $4,000
❑ 1956 Yankees	$800 – $1,200

Ticket Stubs

Although printed in mass quantities, old ticket stubs are rare. Whole tickets also can be worth twice as much as stubs.

1955 Yankees vs. Dodgers
ticket stub

	Values
❑ 1921 Yankees	$450 – $700
❑ 1921 Giants	$450 – $550
❑ 1922 Yankees	$450 – $700
❑ 1923 Giants	$450 – $550
❑ 1923 Yankees	$450 – $700
❑ 1936 Giants	$150 – $225
❑ 1937 Yankees	$150 – $200
❑ 1941 Dodgers	$125 – $225
❑ 1947 Dodgers	$125 – $225
❑ 1949 Dodgers	$125 – $225
❑ 1951 Yankees	$100 – $150
❑ 1952 Dodgers	$120 – $200
❑ 1955 Dodgers	$150 – $300
❑ 1956 Dodgers	$95 – $120
❑ 1956 Yankees	$65 – $125

Uniforms

Game-worn Subway Series uniforms are rare treasures, as are hats and shoes. Most values listed here are appraisals by Sotheby's auction house.

	Values
❏ 1940s Hugh Casey road jersey (Dodgers)	$2,500 – $3,500
❏ 1947 Bill Bevens road uniform (Yankees)	$2,000 – $3,000
❏ 1951 Joe DiMaggio signed final season home pants (Yankees)	$800 – $1,200
❏ 1951 Willie Mays signed rookie road jersey (Giants)	$25,000 – $35,000
❏ 1951 Phil Rizzuto signed road jersey (Yankees)	$2,500 – $3,500
❏ 1953 Johnny Podres signed home jersey (Dodgers)	$1,500 – $2,500
❏ 1956 Mickey Mantle signed road jersey (Yankees)	$25,000 – $35,000
❏ 1956 Billy Martin signed home jersey (Yankees)	$800 – $1,200

Photo taken at the National Baseball Hall of Fame

Jackie Robinson's
Dodgers hat

Bats

Every year, each of the World Series players is given a commemorative black bat with each team member's inscribed signature.

	Values
❏ 1936 Giants	$1,000 – $1,500
❏ 1936 Yankees	$1,500 – $3,000
❏ 1937 Giants	$800 – $1,200
❏ 1937 Yankees	$1,500 – $2,500
❏ 1941 Dodgers	$750 – $1,200
❏ 1941 Yankees	$900 – $1,500
❏ 1947 Dodgers	$500 – $800
❏ 1947 Yankees	$500 – $750
❏ 1949 Dodgers	$500 – $750
❏ 1949 Yankees	$450 – $650
❏ 1951 Giants	$750 – $900
❏ 1951 Yankees	$800 – $1,500
❏ 1952 Dodgers	$550 – $700
❏ 1952 Yankees	$450 – $650
❏ 1953 Dodgers	$550 – $700
❏ 1953 Yankees	$375 – $500

1953 Dodgers black bat

Team-Signed Baseballs

There is something magical about a signed baseball, especially one that has all the signatures of all the team members from a World Series game! Ideally, the top player signs his autograph on the "sweet spot" of the ball, which is the long, narrow stretch between the stitching.

1953 Dodgers baseball with Jackie Robinson's autograph on the "sweet spot"

1955 Dodgers baseball signed on the "sweet spot"

Courtesy of the Seth Swirsky Collection

	Values
❑ 1921 Giants	$2,000 – $3,000
❑ 1921 Yankees	$3,000 – $5,000
❑ 1922 Giants	$2,000 – $3,000
❑ 1922 Yankees	$2,000 – $3,200
❑ 1923 Giants	$2,000 – $3,000
❑ 1923 Yankees	$2,500 – $3,500
❑ 1936 Giants	$600 – $750
❑ 1936 Yankees	$1,000 – $2,000
❑ 1937 Giants	$500 – $750
❑ 1937 Yankees	$1,500 – $2,500
❑ 1941 Dodgers	$500 – $1,000
❑ 1941 Yankees	$800 – $1,200
❑ 1947 Dodgers	$900 – $1,200
❑ 1947 Yankees	$1,000 – $1,200
❑ 1949 Dodgers	$800 – $1,200
❑ 1949 Yankees	$1,200 – $1,500
❑ 1951 Giants	$800 – $1,200
❑ 1951 Yankees	$3,000 – $4,500
❑ 1952 Dodgers	$650 – $900
❑ 1952 Yankees	$750 – $1,000
❑ 1953 Dodgers	$800 – $1,000
❑ 1953 Yankees	$800 – $1,200
❑ 1955 Dodgers	$3,000 – $4,000
❑ 1955 Yankees	$800 – $1,000
❑ 1956 Dodgers	$800 – $1,000
❑ 1956 Yankees	$800 – $1,200

World Series Press Pins

These hard-to-find items are the actual pins used to designate members of the press who attended each of the New York Subway Series. Each team produced its own press pins, except in 1921, 1922 and 1923, when one pin was used for both teams. As with the World Series programs, Dodgers pins tend to command higher values even when they did not win the championship.

	Values
❑ 1921 Yankees/Giants	$2,500 – $4,000
❑ 1923 Yankees/Giants	$2,500 – $4,000
❑ 1947 Dodgers	$600 – $800
❑ 1947 Yankees	$500 – $750
❑ 1956 Dodgers	$800 – $1,500
❑ 1956 Yankees	$200 – $300

1949 Yankees press pin

World Series Rings

One of the rarest and most valuable of all baseball collectibles are the World Series rings. Rings might be the most personal of collectibles and can command nearly any price, which has been noted the few times they have been offered for sale. The values listed here are appraisals by Sotheby's auction house.

	Values
❑ 1936 Earle Combs (Yankees, 14K)	$8,000 – $12,000
❑ 1951 Johnny Hopp (Yankees, 14K)	$3,000 – $5,000
❑ 1951 Joe DiMaggio (Yankees, 10K)	$25,000 – $50,000
❑ 1952 Bob Kuzava (Yankees, 14K)	$3,000 – $5,000
❑ 1956 Mickey Mantle (Yankees, 14K)	$50,000 – $75,000

1956 Yankees
World Series ring

1951 Bowman Leo Durocher
trading card

1952 Bowman Carl Furillo
trading card

1953 Bowman Yogi Berra,
Hank Bauer and Mickey Mantle
trading card

World Series Players Trading Cards

The 13 New York Subway Series featured some of the best players in baseball history. Baseball cards devoted to these players from the Subway Series years, such as Jackie Robinson's 1955 Topps card and Eddie Stanky's 1951 Topps All-Star card, would be great additions to any New York baseball card collection.

Values

Dodgers

❑ 1941 Play Ball
Pee Wee Reese #54 . . . . . $200 – $700

❑ 1955 Topps
Jackie Robinson #50 . . . . $200 – $350

❑ 1956 Topps
Gil Hodges #145 . . . . $35 – $60

Giants

❑ 1937 Goudey Thum Movies
Mel Ott #3 . . . . $100 – $200

❑ 1951 Topps Current All-Stars
Eddie Stanky #11 . . . $5,000 – $13,000

Yankees

❑ 1949 Leaf
Tommy Henrich #55 . . . . $350 – $500

❑ 1952 Bowman
Yogi Berra #1 . . . . $300 – $600

❑ 1952 Topps
Bill Dickey #400 . . . . $500 – $850

❑ 1953 Bowman Yogi Berra,
Hank Bauer and
Mickey Mantle #44 . . . . . $550 – $750

❑ 1955 Bowman
Don Larsen #67 . . . . $10 – $30

New York Baseball Memorabilia
1903 – Present Day

As with Subway Series memorabilia, collectibles devoted to the Yankees and Mets come in all shapes, sizes and values. Among the more common items that have been produced over the years are trading cards, photos, pennants and game programs. Of course, even these common items can have great value if they're connected to a memorable game, such as Game 6 of the 1986 World Series or Babe Ruth's last game, or if they've been signed by such greats as Mickey Mantle, Joe DiMaggio, Tom Seaver or Mike Piazza.

Derek Jeter
Salvino's Bammer

On the second tier, there are special edition posters and comic books, bobbing head dolls and rare and perishable items such as scorecards. Music afficionados can try to put together a collection of great Mets- or Yankees-related tunes, while collectors who are kids at heart will enjoy the many different plush toys and games.

1975 Mets yearbook

Finally, there are the unique and unusual items, which run the gamut from the highly valuable to the slightly bizarre. These memorabilia include stadium objects, such as seats and phones, as well as personal items that belonged to players, such as their World Series rings or even their underwear!

1954 Billy Martin
trading card

Of course, the collectibles rules concerning age and condition apply to New York baseball memorabilia as well. But as to which items have value, there may be no rules at all!

Trading Cards

Given the rich heritage of New York baseball, trading card collectors have almost limitless ways to put together a collection – by year, team, player or any other way under the sun! The earliest cards were printed on heavy cardboard with poor-quality photographs and drawings, unlike the colorful, glossy cards that are produced today. Here is a sampling of cards available that feature past and present Yankees and Mets players, including rookie cards, chrome cards and special commemorative editions.

1962 Topps Joe Torre
trading card

1995 Upper Deck Derek Jeter
trading card

Values

Rookie Cards Of Subway Series Players

❑ 1962 Topps Joe Torre
#218 (Brewers) . . . . $22 – $45

❑ 1971 Topps Bob Valentine
#188 Dodgers Rookies
(Dodgers). . . . . $1.75 – $4

❑ 1985 Donruss Roger Clemens
#273 (Red Sox) . . . . $22 – $45

❑ 1986 Donruss Paul O'Neill
#37 (Rated Rookie, Reds) . . . . $2 – $6

❑ 1987 Topps Traded Tiffany
David Cone #24T (Mets) . . . . . $4 – $8

❑ 1988 Score Rookie Al Leiter
#97T (Yankees) . . . . $1.25 – $3.25

❑ 1990 Topps Bernie Williams
#701 (Yankees) . . . . $.75 – $1.75

❑ 1992 Bowman Mike Hampton
#638 (Mariners) . . . . $4 – $8

❑ 1992 Bowman Mariano Rivera
#302 (Yankees) . . . . $4 – $10

❑ 1993 Upper Deck SP Derek Jeter
#279 (Yankees) . . . . $55 – $110

❑ 1998 Bowman Chrome Orlando
Hernandez #221 (Yankees) . . $4 – $10

❑ 1999 Bowman Chrome Benny
Agbayani #429 (Mets) . . . . $1.50 – $4

Values

Other Cards
Of Yankees Players

☐ 1940 Play Ball
Joe DiMaggio #1 .... $3,000 – $8,000

☐ 1952 Topps Mickey
Mantle #311 ..... $10,000 – $20,000

☐ 1952 Topps Phil Rizzuto
#11 .... $150 – $325

☐ 1956 Topps Yogi Berra
#110................. $75 – $150

☐ 1966 Topps Roger Maris
#365.................. $25 – $50

☐ 1989 Upper Deck
Don Mattingly #200 .... $.75 – $1.75

☐ 1999 Upper Deck Paul
O'Neill #156 .... $.15 – $.30

☐ 1999 Fleer Mystique
Andy Pettitte #17........ $.10 – $.25

Other Cards
Of Mets Players

☐ 1969 Topps Nolan Ryan
#533................ $150 – $325

☐ 1970 Topps Tom Seaver
#300.................. $15 – $35

☐ 1986 Donruss Highlights
Dwight Gooden #8 ...... $.20 – $.50

☐ 1987 Leaf/Donruss
Len Dykstra #88 .... $.05 – $.15

☐ 1989 Upper Deck
Keith Hernandez #612.... $.10 – $.30

☐ 1994 Upper Deck
John Franco #323 .... $.10 – $.25

☐ 1998 Donruss Preferred
Robin Ventura #82 ...... $.10 – $.25

☐ 1998 Pinnacle Museum Collection
John Olerud #PP35 .... $1.25 – $2.75

circa 1957 Topps Mickey Mantle
and Yogi Berra Power Hitters
trading card

1963 Topps Don Zimmer
trading card

1967 Topps Tom Seaver
trading card

Signed Baseballs

A signed baseball is pretty special, but even more so when it's signed by an entire World Series team, connected to a memorable moment or is the only one of its kind. There are many treasures to choose from, from a relatively common ball signed by Don Mattingly to a one-of-a-kind item such as Babe Ruth's last signed ball.

Mookie Wilson signed baseball

Babe Ruth signed baseball

Rey Ordonez signed baseball

Values

Yankees

- ❑ David Cone . . . . $25 – $30
- ❑ Joe and Norma Jean DiMaggio . . . . $20,000 – $30,000
- ❑ Lou Gehrig. . . . . $2,500 – $3,500
- ❑ Don Mattingly . . . . $45 – $55

Mets

- ❑ Willie Mays . . . . $40 – $50
- ❑ Mike Piazza . . . . $35 – $65
- ❑ Tom Seaver . . . . $40 – $50
- ❑ Mookie Wilson (ball Wilson hit through Bill Buckner's legs in the 1986 World Series, Game 6). . $63,000

Team-Signed Baseballs

- ❑ 1920 Yankees . . . . . . $2,800 – $3,200
- ❑ 1923 Yankees . . . . . . $3,000 – $3,500
- ❑ 1937 Yankees . . . . . . $1,000 – $2,000
- ❑ 1955 Yankees . . . . $800 – $1,000
- ❑ 1964 Mets . . . . $400 – $500
- ❑ 1968 Mets . . . . $600 – $700
- ❑ 1969 Mets . . . . $1,500 – $2,500
- ❑ 1986 Mets . . . . $400 – $475
- ❑ 1988 Yankees . . . . $175 – $225
- ❑ 1992 Mets . . . . $80 – $100
- ❑ 1995 Yankees . . . . $90 – $110

Yankees

Values

- ❏ 1956 Yankees,
  team-signed . . . . $3,000 – $3,500
- ❏ Yogi Berra, game-used . $500 – $1,000
- ❏ Lou Gehrig $10,000
- ❏ Mickey Mantle. . . . . . . $500 – $2,000
- ❏ Joe Torre . . . . $30 – $60
- ❏ Dave Winfield $100– $200

Mets

- ❏ 1969 Mets, team-signed . $400 – $500
- ❏ Keith Hernandez. . . . . . . $50 – $100
- ❏ Cleon Jones . . . . $20 – $75
- ❏ Jerry Koosman . . . . $50 – $100
- ❏ Tug McGraw . . . . $20 – $75

Signed Bats

Much like signed baseballs, signed bats come in all types, with all sorts of collector value attached to them.

Phil Rizzuto signed bat

Yankees

Values

- ❏ Bill Dickey stamped
  store model glove . . . . $50 – $125
- ❏ Whitey Ford stamped store
  model left-handed glove . . . $45 – $85
- ❏ Lou Gehrig stamped store
  model left-handed glove. $900 – $1,200
- ❏ Don Larsen stamped
  store model glove . . . . $40 – $85
- ❏ Phil Rizzuto signed rookie
  game-used glove . . . . $2,500 – $3,000

Mets

- ❏ Gil Hodges stamped
  store model glove . . . . $45 – $95
- ❏ Tom Seaver stamped
  store model glove . . . . $75 – $120

Signed Gloves

Because most gloves have stamped signatures, the key to their collectibility is the number of gloves produced in that particular style.

Bill Dickey signed catcher's mitt

Tom Seaver's 1969
World Series Jersey

Joe DiMaggio's 1937 hat

Yogi Berra's signed jersey

Uniforms

For the right price, collectors can acquire uniforms worn by some of the greatest Yankees and Mets. Many of these items have been signed and are among the most valuable items around today.

Values

Yankees

❑ 1935 Babe Ruth
home uniform..... $25,000 – $50,000

❑ 1944 Bill Bevens
game-worn cap......... $400 – $600

❑ 1948 Joe DiMaggio
signed home jersey . $15,000 – $20,000

❑ 1957 Enos Slaughter
signed home jersey ... $1,500 – $2,500

❑ 1961 Roger Maris
road pants .... $2,000 – $3,000

❑ 1967 Mickey Mantle
signed home pants ... $1,500 – $2,000

❑ 1970 Bill Burbach
home jersey .... $500 – $1,000

❑ 1994 Don Mattingly
road jersey.......... $800 – $1,200

Mets

❑ 1963-65 Casey Stengel
manager's road jersey. $8,000 – $12,000

❑ 1970 Jerry Koosman
signed road jersey .... $2,000 – $3,000

❑ 1973 Willie Mays
signed road jersey .... $2,500 – $3,500

❑ 1983 Tom Seaver
signed warm-up jacket. $1,000 – $2,000

❑ 1984 Dwight Gooden
signed home jersey..... $800 – $1,200

Press Pins

The pins used to identify members of the press at sporting events have become quite popular in recent years, due in part to their limited availability. Rarer still are the "phantom" pins, which were produced for teams believed to have a chance at making a Series but don't.

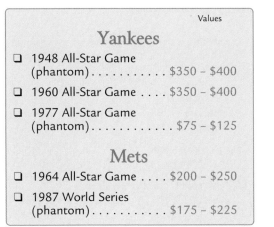

Values

Yankees

❑ 1948 All-Star Game
(phantom) . . . . $350 – $400

❑ 1960 All-Star Game . . . . $350 – $400

❑ 1977 All-Star Game
(phantom) . . . . $75 – $125

Mets

❑ 1964 All-Star Game . . . . $200 – $250

❑ 1987 World Series
(phantom) . . . . $175 – $225

1973 Mets press pin

Yearbooks

Chock full of features, photos and stats, yearbooks are a big part of nostalgic Yankees and Mets memorabilia. Yearbooks from notable years in the team's history, such as the Yankees' yearbook from 1968 (Mickey Mantle's last year), are particularly coveted by collectors.

Values

Yankees

❑ 1950 First Year,
Big League Books. . . . . . $250 – $350

❑ 1982 . . . . $5 – $12

❑ 1985 Maris, Mantle,
Ruth, Gehrig . . . . $5 – $12

Mets

❑ 1962 First Year. . . . . $300 – $350

❑ 1987 World Champions
logo . . . . $10 – $15

1975 Mets yearbook

October 3,1955 *Daily News*

July 19,1999 *Daily News*

July 19,1999 *The New York Times*

Headlines

Sometimes the headlines that celebrate New York's greatest baseball moments are as memorable as the events themselves. In fact, collecting headlines has grown in popularity in recent years.

Values

Yankees

❑ December 17, 1933
The Daily Ghost, "Babe Retires," signed . . . . . $2,000 – $3,000

❑ July 1936 *Time,*
Joe DiMaggio. . . . . $300 – $500

❑ November/December 1956
Baseball Digest, Don Larsen . . $10 – $20

❑ October 1, 1956 *Sports Illustrated,* Mickey Mantle, World Series . . . . $50 – $75

❑ February 1977 *Baseball Digest,*
Thurman Munson . . . . $5 – $8

❑ December 1996 *Baseball Digest,* Derek Jeter . . . . $2 – $5

Mets

❑ December 22, 1969 *Sports Illustrated,* Tom Seaver. . . . . . $25 – $40

❑ April 13, 1970 *Sports Illustrated,*
Jerry Koosman. . . . . $5 – $15

❑ June 21, 1971 *Sports Illustrated,*
Jerry Grote. . . . . $5 – $10

❑ January 1981 *Baseball Digest,*
Tug McGraw . . . . $4 – $6

❑ April 7, 1986 *Time,*
Dwight Gooden. . . . . $10 – $15

❑ March 23, 1993 *Sports Illustrated,* Dwight Gooden . . . . $3 – $5

Other Products

Collectors can find all sorts of products with New York ballplayers on them. Recently, cereal boxes featuring the faces of famous sluggers have grown in popularity, so their values have risen on the secondary market. Other products include soda cans emblazoned with both players' names and team insignias. As usual, signed items are head and shoulders above all the others and are valued accordingly.

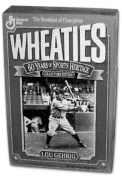

1992 Lou Gehrig
Wheaties box

	Values
Yankees	
❑ 1937 Joe DiMaggio Wheaties box	$175 – $250
❑ 1967-1968 Mel Stottlemyre Coca-Cola bottle cap	$2 – $4
❑ 1977 Thurman Munson Royal Crown Cola can. . . .	$2.50 – $6
❑ 1980s Mickey Mantle Wheaties box, signed . .	$750 – $1000
❑ 1992 Babe Ruth Wheaties box	$8 – $15
❑ 1992 Lou Gehrig Wheaties box	$8 – $15
❑ 1996 Yankees Championship Wheaties box	$12 – $18
Mets	
❑ 1967-1968 Ed Kranepool Coca-Cola bottle cap . . .	$1.25 – 2.75
❑ 1977 Tom Seaver Royal Crown Cola can	$6 – $12
❑ 1997 Ryne Sandberg/ Cal Ripken Jr./Mike Piazza Wheaties box	$10 – $15

1986 Mets
Royal Crown Cola can

Advertising

It's only natural that the biggest names in baseball would endorse products and that these rare advertisements would be coveted by collectors.

1935 Babe Ruth
Quaker Puffed Wheat Or Rice Ad

Values

Yankees

❑ 1927 Babe Ruth and Lou Gehrig tour ad w/stop in Fresno, California .... $10,000 – $15,000

❑ 1935 Babe Ruth Quaker Puffed Wheat Or Rice ad w/free gifts pictured .... N/E

❑ April 17, 1937 *Time* ad w/Lou Gehrig Camels cartoon. $35 – $50

❑ *circa* 1962 Gold Mine Icicles ad poster w/Roger Maris at bat, signed .... $500 – $1,000

Mets

❑ 1960s official Mets wristwatch ad w/Mr. Met and order form .... $15 – $25

Stadium Memorabilia

Those who want to own a piece of history have found value in turnstiles, seats and bricks from renovated stadiums.

Courtesy of the Seth Swirsky Collection

Original Yankees
Stadium seat

Values

Yankee Stadium

❑ Brick from the 1973 remodeling .... $100 – $200

❑ Stadium seats, double............ $1,200 – $1,500

❑ Stadium seat, single ... $900 – $1,250

❑ Ticket stub deposit box (cylindrical metal w/slot and handles) .... $400 – $600

❑ Turnstile .... $1,500 – $2,000

Shea Stadium

❑ Stadium seats, double............ $1,200 – $1,500

❑ Usher's navy blue wool jacket .... $400 – $600

Unusual Items

These special baseball-related items will impress even the most casual fan. Many values listed below reflect appraisals from auction houses, while the values of other items have not yet been established.

Values

❏ December 26, 1919 contract
w/transfer of Babe Ruth from
Red Sox to Yankees . . . . N/E

❏ 1930s Babe Ruth-brand
white cotton underwear $200

❏ Early 1950s photograph of Marilyn
Monroe in a batting pose, signed,
w/comments about her husband,
Joe DiMaggio. . . . . $20,000 – $30,000

❏ September 9, 1950 minor league
Yankee affiliate paycheck to Mickey
Mantle, endorsed . . . $1,500 – $2,000

❏ September 1964 harmonica played
by Phil Linz on the team bus after the
Yankees lost a double-header in Chicago.
Irritated by the noise, manager Yogi
Berra knocked the harmonica from
Linz' mouth. This became a turning
point for the team who later won the
pennant over Chicago . $500 – $1,000

❏ August 15, 1965 baseball signed
by the Beatles during a concert at
Shea Stadium . . . . N/E

❏ Late 1960s toothpick found in
Tom Seaver's warm-up jacket
w/letter of authenticity $400

❏ June 28, 1969 miniature brass
rocking chair given to Heinie
Manush on Old Timers' Day
w/letter of authenticity . . $200 – $400

❏ Late 1970s to early 1980s
sealed box of 36 "Reggie"
candy bars w/original
advertising and box displays $600

1930s Babe Ruth-brand
cotton underwear box

Yankees World Championship
bracelet that Joe McCarthy
gave to his wife, Babe

1965 baseball autographed at
Shea Stadium by the Beatles:
George Harrison, John Lennon,
Paul McCartney and Ringo Star

Ticket Stubs

Fans who didn't have the chance to attend the great games in the teams' histories can console themselves with ticket stubs from those games!

1999 Yankees vs. Expos ticket

Values

Yankees

❑ 1932 Ruth's "Called Shot"
Game 3, World Series . $2,500 – $3,000

❑ 1969 Mickey Mantle Day. $900 – $1,200

❑ 1976 American League
Championship Series . . . . . . $10 – $25

Mets

❑ April 13, 1962 first Polo
Grounds home game . . . $800 – $1,100

❑ 1969 National League
Championship Series . . . . . . $25 – $50

❑ April 18, 1981 Tom
Seaver's 3,000th strikeout . $100 – $175

❑ August 4, 1985
Tom Seaver's 300th win . . $100 – $125

❑ 1986 National League
Championship Series . . . . . . $10 – $20

Media Guides

Media guides are more than books of statistics. They can be very popular if they are from a year in which something notable occurred.

1984 Mets media guide

Values

Yankees

❑ 1927 Roster. . . . . $150 – $200

❑ 1942 Joe McCarthy . . . . . . $60 – $75

❑ 1960 Yankee Stadium . . . . $80 – $100

❑ 1975 Bobby Bonds/
Catfish Hunter . . . . $15 – $30

❑ 1992 Great Moments . . . . . $12 – $18

Mets

❑ 1962 First Year. . . . . $400 – $600

❑ 1965 Mascot. . . . . $80 – $100

❑ 1971 Scoreboard. . . . . $45 – $60

❑ 1986 Dwight Gooden/
Shea Stadium . . . . $12 – $18

❑ 1993 Uniform . . . . $12 – $18

Bobbin' Heads

A "golden age" collectible, bobbin' head dolls have been part of baseball's memorabilia landscape since the 1960s. Many different types of Yankees and Mets bobbin' head dolls have been made over the years, with the older, more delicate papier-maché head designs generally being the most valuable to sports memorabilia collectors. Some pieces have been produced with different colors, logos and base shapes, so collectors may want to find these variations.

1990s Derek Jeter
bobbin' head

	Values
Yankees	
☐ 1960-1961 boy's head (orange square base)	$100 – $150
☐ 1962-1964 boy's head (green round base, black player)	$1,100 – $1,500
☐ 1961-1962 Mickey Mantle (small)	$800 – $1,200
☐ 1961-1962 Roger Maris (large)	$450 – $625
☐ Lou Gehrig (porcelain)	$40 – $70
Mets	
☐ 1960-1961 boy's head (blue square base)	$180 – $200
☐ 1961-1962 boy's head (white square base)	$225 – $325
☐ 1965-1972 boy's head (gold round base)	$65 – $85
☐ 1969 Mr. and Mrs. Met (gold round base)	$225 – $300
☐ Nolan Ryan (porcelain)	$65 – $85

1990s Tom Seaver
bobbin' head

Pennants

Vintage New York pennants were made of felt, so finding one in good condition may be a tough task for today's sports enthusiasts.

1990s Mets pennant

Yankees

Values

☐ 1940s Joe DiMaggio, signed (blue & white) . . $800 – $1,200

☐ 1940s Joe DiMaggio (red & white w/Yankee Clipper) . . . . . . $200 – $400

☐ 1969 Mickey Mantle Day at Yankee Stadium . . . . $65 – $150

☐ 1991-1992 Don Mattingly . . . $5 – $10

Mets

☐ 1969 Mets World Champs (orange on blue) . . . . $90 – $175

☐ 1994 Miracle Mets 25th Anniversary . . . . $10 – $15

Signed Photos

If a picture is worth a thousand words, then shots of great Mets and Yankees players with their autographs are worth a lot more!

David Cone signed photo

Yankees

Values

☐ 1927 Babe Ruth and Lou Gehrig . . . . $8,000 – $12,000

☐ 1939 Yankees . . . . $3,000 – $5,000

☐ Joe DiMaggio . . . . $150 – $300

☐ Whitey Ford . . . . $15 – $25

☐ Chuck Knoblauch . . . . $20 – $30

☐ Roger Maris . . . . $300 – $500

Mets

☐ 1969 Mets celebration . . . . $60 – $150

☐ Willie Mays . . . . $30 – $60

☐ Mike Piazza . . . . $30 – $55

Programs, Schedules & Scorecards

Old programs can be hard to find in good condition, as an exciting game can wreak havoc with a paper program (to say nothing of mustard and ketchup stains).

Values

Yankees Programs

❑ 1926 Yankees vs. Cardinals
World Series . . . . $2,000 – $3,000

❑ 1939 American League
All-Star Game . . . . $800 – $1,500

❑ 1960 American League
All-Star Game #2 . . . . $80 – $125

❑ 1976 American League
Playoff Game . . . . $10 – $20

❑ 1977 American League
All-Star Game . . . . $10 – $30

❑ 1981 American League
Playoff Game . . . . $10 – $20

Mets Programs

❑ 1964 National League
All-Star Game . . . . $225 – $300

❑ 1969 National League
Playoff Game . . . . $200 – $325

❑ 1973 National League
Playoff Game . . . . $50 – $100

❑ 1986 National League
Playoff Game . . . . $15 – $30

Schedule

❑ 1924 American League
pocket schedule $50

Lineup Card

❑ October 10, 1961 Yankees
Lineup Card w/Mickey
Mantle, Roger Maris and
Yogi Berra . . . . $500 – $700

1964 Mets program

1971 Mets scorecard

1985 Yankees schedule

Posters

Baseball posters have become popular memorabilia items that, in some cases, can command quite a price, depending on their age and condition. Sports fans may choose posters that feature favorite players or ones that honor the whole team.

Tino Martinez poster

Values

Yankees

❑ 1968 Mickey Mantle . . . . $175 – $225
❑ 1968 Mel Stottlemyre . . . . . $10 – $15
❑ 1968-1971 Bobby Murcer . . $10 – $16

Mets

❑ 1968 Buddy Harrelson. . . . . $10 – $15
❑ 1969 Let's Go Mets . . . . $30 – $45
❑ 1968 Tom Seaver. . . . . $70 – $90

Comic Books

Some of New York's greatest ballplayers have been captured in comic book form over the years, much to the delight of younger fans.

1991 comic book with Mickey Mantle cover

Values

Yankees

❑ Oct. 1940 *Sport Comics* w/Lou Gehrig story (#1) . $250 – $325
❑ May 1948 *True Comics* w/Joe DiMaggio cover (#71). $50 – $150
❑ 1951 *Phil Rizzuto Baseball Hero* w/Rizzuto cover . . . . $300 – $400
❑ 1952 *Thrilling True Story of Baseball* w/Yankees cover. . $350 – $550
❑ Dec. 1991 *Magnum Comics* w/Mickey Mantle (#1) . . . . . . $5 – $15

Mets

❑ April 1949 *Babe Ruth Sports Comics,* w/Yogi Berra. . . . . $110 – $140
❑ Sept. 1954 *The Amazing Willie Mays* . . . . $350 – $450

Values

Yankees

- ❏ "Babe Ruth: The Home Run King" by A.L. Burt Co. (1920). . . . . $350 – $425

- ❏ "The Magnificent Yankees" by Tom Meany (1952) . . . . . $35 – $65

- ❏ "Yogi Berra – The Muscle Man" by Ben Epstein (1951) . . . . $150 – $250

Mets

- ❏ "Backstage at the Mets" by Lindsey Nelson and Al Hirshberg (1966). . . . . $30 – $45

- ❏ "We Won Today: My Season with the Mets" by Kathryn Parker (1977) . . . . $30 – $45

Books

Book collectors and sports fans will love these books celebrating the heritage of New York baseball. The values listed are for first editions.

"The Amazing Mets"
by Jerry Mitchell

Values

Recordings

- ❏ "The Amazing Mets" (1969 season recap). . . . . . . $20 – $30

- ❏ "I Love Mickey" (1956, 45 rpm, sung by Theresa Brewer) . . $75 – $100

- ❏ "That Holler Guy" (1964, 45 rpm, by Joe Garagiola). $100 – $200

- ❏ "Take Me Out to the Ballgame" (sung by the Yankees) . . . . $200 – $400

Sheet Music

- ❏ "Batterin' Babe" (1919). . $300 – $500

- ❏ "I Can't Get To First Base With You" (1935, by Eleanor Gehrig & Fred Fisher) . $1,500 – $2,500

- ❏ "Joltin' Joe DiMaggio" (1941) . . . . $1,000 – $1,500

Music

Collectors with a passion for music will relish finding both recordings and sheet music for some of baseball's best-known ditties.

1941 "Joltin' Joe DiMaggio"
sheet music

Plush Toys

These adorable little guys are popular with plush collectors and memorabilia hunters alike. In addition to relatively common plush, there have been special Beanie Babies given away at baseball games that are great commemoratives.

Valentino™ Beanie Baby®

	Values
Yankees	
❑ Valentino™ *Beanie Baby®* by Ty®, the only *Beanie Baby* to be exhibited at the Baseball Hall of Fame. It was the giveaway on May 17, 1998, the night David Wells pitched a perfect game	$100 – $115
❑ Yankees bear by North American Bear Company	$40 – $60
Mets	
❑ Mike Piazza plush doll	$16 – $20

Games & Toys

A growing segment of the sports memorabilia market are toys and games. Yankees and Mets superstars have been featured on several different types of toys and games over the years, with the oldest items having the greatest value.

1998 Mets die-cast truck

	Values
Yankees	
❑ *circa* 1930 Babe Ruth Baseball Game	$700 – $900
❑ *circa* 1930 Lou Gehrig's Official Playball	$700 – $1,000
Mets	
❑ 1970 Gil Hodges Pennant Fever	$125– $200
❑ 1954 Say Hey! Willie Mays Baseball Game	$400 – $650

Figurines

One person's toy is another person's collectible, especially for older items. Figurines depicting New York baseball stars have been produced for years, but most are of fairly recent vintage. Still, many of these had limited distribution and are hard to find in good condition. Some of the items below are unusual, such as the Bill Dickey artist's proof.

1992 Don Mattingly figurine

Values

Yankees

❑ David Cone, Kenner Starting
Lineup (Mets uniform). . . . . $30 – $50

❑ Bill Dickey, ProSport
Creations, artist's proof . . $90 – $125

❑ Joe DiMaggio, Gartlan,
artist's proof . . . . $6,000 – $8,000

❑ Whitey Ford, Hartland . . . $75 – $110

❑ Orlando Hernandez,
Kenner Starting Lineup . . . . $15 – $25

❑ Mickey Mantle/Roger Maris,
Kenner Starting Lineup
Baseball Classic Doubles . . . $15 – $30

❑ Roger Maris, Salvino Inc. . . $70 – $125

❑ Thurman Munson,
Sports Impressions (7") . . . $70 – $100

Mets

❑ Rey Ordonez,
Kenner Starting Lineup . . . . $20 – $30

❑ Mike Piazza, Sports
Impressions, signed
(Dodgers uniform, 7") . . . $100 – $150

❑ Darryl Strawberry,
Gartlan mini-figurine . . . . . . $30 – $50

1997 Derek Jeter figurine

1999 Mike Piazza figurine

Ballpark Souvenirs

Mets mini helmet

Yankees charm bracelet

Mets pennant set

Items that are only available on game days are a natural for memorabilia collectors, as are items available at ballpark souvenir stands. These can include everything from pencils in the shape of baseball bats to commemorative plates, to say nothing of the renowned "souvenir cup!" While they're popular with collectors for their sentimental value, a few pieces have soared in value on the secondary market.

Values

Yankees

- ❑ 25-Time World Series
  Champions banner . . . . $50 – $65

- ❑ 1937 Yankees visor
  w/baseball logo . . . . $50 – $55

- ❑ 1940s Joe DiMaggio
  pencil bat . . . . $80 – $100

- ❑ 1947 World Series
  pin w/team portrait . . . . . $700 – $800

- ❑ 1956 World Series plate
  commemorating Don
  Larsen's perfect game . . . . $80 – $150

- ❑ 1960s popcorn
  holder/megaphone . . . . $25 – $40

- ❑ 1970s souvenir cup . . . . $5 – $15

- ❑ 1999 World Series bear . . . . $15 – $20

- ❑ Yogi Berra stadium photo
  pin (blue background) . . . . . $50 – $65

- ❑ Lou Gehrig mechanical pencil
  bat w/image of Gehrig . . . . . $50 – $60

- ❑ Mickey Mantle "Champion
  Slugger" kids T-shirt . . . . . $250 – $325

- ❑ Babe Ruth knife keychain . . $75 – $100

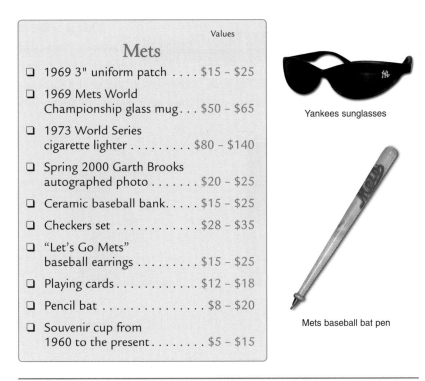

Mets

Values

- 1969 3" uniform patch . . . . $15 – $25
- 1969 Mets World Championship glass mug. . . $50 – $65
- 1973 World Series cigarette lighter . . . . $80 – $140
- Spring 2000 Garth Brooks autographed photo . . . . $20 – $25
- Ceramic baseball bank. . . . . $15 – $25
- Checkers set . . . . $28 – $35
- "Let's Go Mets" baseball earrings . . . . $15 – $25
- Playing cards . . . . $12 – $18
- Pencil bat . . . . $8 – $20
- Souvenir cup from 1960 to the present . . . . $5 – $15

Yankees sunglasses

Mets baseball bat pen

Acknowledgements

CheckerBee Publishing extends a special thanks to the many collectors and retailers who contributed their valuable time to assist us with this book, including Chris Altieri, Sue and Dennis Bacon, James Baird, Lee Ballard, Baseball Hall of Fame (*Cooperstown, N.Y.*), Frank Cahill, Tim Cammett (*Diamond Images, Alexandria, Va.*), Bruce DiCarlo (*BJN Collectibles, Worcester, Mass.*), Rick Fiallo (*Mets Clubhouse, Manhattan*), Greg Fisher (*Cameo Enterprises, Youngstown, N.Y.*), Bob and Janice Johnson (*The Vintage Zone, Scottsdale, Ariz.*), JQ's Slous (*Providence, R,.I.*), George Kanellopoulos (*Yankees Clubhouse, Times Square, Manhattan*), Michael N. Klar, Steve Levy (*Brooklyn Boy Cards and Sports Memorabilia, Ramsey, N.J.*), Mark and Judy McGuinness, Barbara Mills, Joseph Morell, Jo Ann Piebenga (*Black Hawk Flea Market, Black Hawk, S.D.*), Sherry Small, Wayne Somero (*The Grand Slam, Vernon, Conn.*), Seth Swirsky and Michael Wills.

The Best Of The Bronx

This is a list of Yankees all-time greats, not including any players on the 2000 Yankees' active roster. All of the statistics are listed for the player's entire career (not necessarily all spent with the Yankees).

AP/WWP

Yogi
Berra
Catcher
Stats: .285, 358 HR, 1430 RBI
Inducted to Hall of Fame: 1972
Retired Number: 8 (w/Bill Dickey)
3-Time MVP: 1951, 1954, 1955

AP/WWP

Jack
Chesbro
Pitcher
Stats: 198-132 W-L, 2.68 ERA
Inducted to Hall of Fame: 1946
Nickname: Happy Jack

AP/WWP

Bill
Dickey
Catcher
Stats: .313, 202 HR, 1209 RBI
Inducted to Hall of Fame: 1954
Retired Number: 8 (w/Yogi Berra)

AP/WWP

Joe
DiMaggio
Outfield
Stats: .325, 361 HR, 1537 RBI
Inducted to Hall of Fame: 1955
Retired Number: 5
3-Time MVP: 1939, 1941, 1947

Whitey
Ford
Pitcher
Stats: 236-106 W-L, 2.75 ERA
Inducted to Hall of Fame: 1974
Retired Number: 16
Cy Young Award: 1961

Lou
Gehrig
First Base
Stats: .340, 493 HR, 1995 RBI
Inducted to Hall of Fame: 1939
Retired Number: 4
2-Time MVP: 1927, 1936
Triple Crown: 1934

Lefty
Gomez
Pitcher
Stats: 189-102 W-L, 3.34 ERA
Inducted to Hall of Fame: 1972
Nickname: Goofy

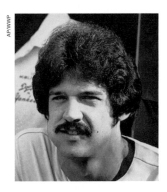

Ron
Guidry
Pitcher
Stats: 170-91 W-L, 3.29 ERA
Cy Young Award: 1978
Nickname: Louisiana Lightning

AP/WWP

Elston
Howard
Catcher
Stats: .274, 167 HR, 762 RBI
Retired Number: 32
MVP: 1963
Note: Became first Yankee to break
color barrier in 1955

AP/WWP

Waite
Hoyt
Pitcher
Stats: 237-182 W-L, 3.59 ERA
Inducted to Hall of Fame: 1969
Nickname: Schoolboy

AP/WWP

Miller
Huggins
Manager
Career Record: 1,413-1,134 W-L
Yankee Record: 1,067-719 W-L
Yankee World Series Titles: 3
Inducted to Hall of Fame: 1964

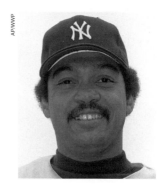

AP/WWP

Reggie
Jackson
Outfield
Stats: .262, 563 HR, 1702 RBI
Inducted to Hall of Fame: 1993
Retired Number: 44
MVP: 1973 (w/Oakland)
Nickname: Mr. October

AP/WWP

Tony
Lazzeri
Second Base
Stats: .292, 178 HR, 1191 RBI
Inducted to Hall of Fame: 1991

AP/WWP

Mickey
Mantle
Outfield
Stats: .298, 536 HR, 1509 RBI
Inducted to Hall of Fame: 1974
Retired Number: 7
3-Time MVP: 1956, 1957, 1962
Triple Crown: 1956

AP/WWP

Roger
Maris
Outfield
Stats: .260, 275 HR, 851 RBI
Retired Number: 9
2-Time MVP: 1960, 1961

AP/WWP

Billy
Martin
Manager
Career Record: 1,253-1,013 W-L
Yankee Record: 556-385 W-L
Yankee World Series Titles: 1
Retired Number: 1

AP/WWP

Don
Mattingly

First Base
Stats: .307, 222 HR, 1099 RBI
Retired Number: 23
MVP: 1985
Nickname: Donnie Baseball

AP/WWP

Joe
McCarthy

Manager
Career Record: 2,125-1,333 W-L
Yankee Record: 1,460-867 W-L
Yankee World Series Titles: 7
Inducted to Hall of Fame: 1957

AP/WWP

Thurman
Munson

Catcher
Stats: .292, 113 HR, 701 RBI
Retired Number: 15
Rookie Of The Year: 1970
MVP: 1976

AP/WWP

Herb
Pennock

Pitcher
Stats: 241-162 W-L, 3.60 ERA
Inducted to Hall of Fame: 1948

AP/WWP

Phil
Rizzuto

Shortstop
Stats: .273, 38 HR, 563 RBI
Inducted to Hall of Fame: 1994
Retired Number: 10
MVP: 1950
Nickname: Scooter

AP/WWP

Babe
Ruth

Outfield
Stats: .342, 714 HR, 2213 RBI
Inducted to Hall of Fame: 1936
Retired Number: 3
MVP: 1923
Nickname: The Sultan of Swat

AP/WWP

Casey
Stengel

Manager
Career Record: 1,905-1,842 W-L
Yankee Record: 1,149-696 W-L
Yankee World Series Titles: 7
Inducted to Hall of Fame: 1966
Retired Number: 37

AP/WWP

Dave
Winfield

Outfield
Stats: .283, 465 HR, 1833 RBI
Eligible for Hall of Fame: 2001

This is a list of Mets all-time greats, not including any players on the 2000 Mets' active roster. All statistics are through the 2000 season. All of the statistics listed are for the player's entire career (not necessarily all spent with the Mets).

Gary
Carter
Catcher
Stats: .262, 324 HR, 1225 RBI
Nickname: The Kid

Dwight
Gooden
Pitcher
Stats: 194-112 W-L, 3.51 ERA
Rookie Of The Year: 1984
Cy Young Award: 1985
Nickname: Doc

Keith
Hernandez
First Base
Stats: .296, 162 HR, 1071 RBI
MVP: 1979 (w/St. Louis)

Jerry
Koosman
Pitcher
Stats: 222-209 W-L, 3.36 ERA
Nickname: Kooz

Tug
McGraw
Pitcher
Stats: 96-92 W-L, 3.14 ERA, 180 Saves
Famous Quote: "You Gotta Believe"
Note: Tug is the father of
country singer Tim McGraw

Tom
Seaver
Pitcher
Stats: 311-205 W-L, 2.86 ERA
Inducted to Hall of Fame: 1992
Retired Number: 41
Rookie Of The Year: 1967
Cy Young Award: 1969, 1973, 1975

Rusty
Staub
Outfield
Stats: .279, 292 HR, 1466 RBI
Nickname: Le Grand Orange

Darryl
Strawberry
Outfield
Stats: .259, 335 HR, 1000 RBI
Rookie Of The Year: 1983

Playing Both Sides
Yankees – Mets Connections

This section showcases the 12 players and coaches who played a role in the 2000 Yankees or Mets season who have had connections with both major league franchises at some point in their career.

David Cone

AllSport

As Player:

New York Mets
1987-1992

New York Yankees
1995-Present

Billy Connors

AP/WWP

As Player:

New York Mets
1967-1968

As Coach:

New York Yankees
1989-1990,
1994-1995

** filled in for
Stottlemyre during
part of 2000 season*

Dwight Gooden

AP/WWP

As Player:

New York Mets
1984-1994

New York Yankees
1996-1997,
2000-Present

Al Leiter

As Player:

New York Yankees
1987-1989

New York Mets
1998-Present

AP/WWP

Lee Mazzilli

AP/WWP

As Player:

New York Mets
1976-1981,
1986-1989

New York Yankees
1982

As Coach:

New York Yankees
2000-Present

Willie Randolph

As Player:

New York Yankees
1976-1988

New York Mets
1992

As Coach:

New York Yankees
1994-Present

AP/WWP

Mel
Stottlemyre

As Player:

New York Yankees
1964-1974

As Coach:

New York Mets
1984-1993

New York Yankees
1996-Present

Ryan
Thompson

As Player:

New York Mets
1992-1995

New York Yankees
2000-Present

Joe
Torre

As Player:

New York Mets
1975-1977

As Manager:

New York Mets
1977-1981

New York Yankees
1996-Present

Jose
Vizcaino

As Player:

New York Mets
1994-1996

New York Yankees
2000-Present

Allen
Watson

As Player:

New York Mets
1999

New York Yankees
1999-Present

Don
Zimmer

As Player:

New York Mets
1962

As Coach:

New York Yankees
1983, 1986,
1996-Present

Other Prominent Yankees-Mets Connections

Managers for both teams: Yogi Berra, Dallas Green, Casey Stengel
Notable players for both teams: Neil Allen, Rickey Henderson, Dave Kingman, Kenny Rogers, Darryl Strawberry, Ralph Terry, Marv Throneberry

Great Moments In Yankees History

There are many great events in the history of the Yankees and we've spotlighted some of the most memorable moments over the last 40 years. You can read about many more great Yankee moments beginning on page 74 in "The Yankees – Team Of The Century" section.

October 1, 1961 – After hitting 39 homers in 1960, Yankees outfielder **Roger Maris** unleashed a season-long power show that put him

AP/WWP

in the record books. By September, Maris had 54 homers and the pressure mounted as he chased Babe Ruth's historic mark of 60 home runs. Maris had 60 as he entered the final game of the season at Yankee Stadium and he drilled a pitch from Red Sox rookie Tracy Stallard into the right field bleachers for his 61st home run.

Roger Maris watches his 61st home run.

October 14, 1976 – A thrilling back-and-forth A.L.C.S. battle between the East champion Yankees and West champion Kansas City Royals came down to the ninth inning. With the score tied 6-6, Yankees first baseman **Chris Chambliss** hit a towering home run just over the fence in right for a series-winning home run, setting off an equally memorable mob scene as fans stormed the field.

AP/WWP

Chris Chambliss is mobbed by fans.

AP/WWP

Reggie Jackson's three amazing homers in 1977.

October 18, 1977 – **Reggie Jackson** put on an amazing power display in Game 6 of the 1977 World Series against the Dodgers. "Mr. October" started the barrage with a two-run homer in the fourth, then one inning later, he whacked another two-run homer. In the eighth inning, Jackson crushed a solo shot to dead center to cement an 8-4 win.

Bucky Dent drives it over the wall.

October 2, 1978 – In July of 1978, the Yankees were 14 games behind first-place Boston, but by September had taken over the top spot in the AL East. Boston tied the Yankees on the last day of the season, forcing a one-game playoff to determine the division title. In the seventh inning, with the Yankees down 2-0 at Fenway Park, light-hitting shortstop Bucky Dent lofted a three-run homer over the Green Monster to lead the Yankees to a dramatic 5-4 win and and clinch a postseason berth.

May 17, 1998 and July 18, 1999 – Not many teams have had a perfect game, let alone two in back-to-back seasons. In 1998, hefty lefty David Wells mastered the Minnesota Twins, with only one tricky grounder in the eighth providing any drama. It was the first Yankees perfect game since Don Larsen's 1956 World Series performance. In the very next season, Yankee pitcher David Cone threw a perfect game against the Montreal Expos.

The Yankees congratulate David Cone.

Luis Sojo smacks his series-clinching single.

October 26, 2000 – Game 5 of the World Series against the New York Mets was tied 2-2 going into the ninth inning. Mets lefty Al Leiter struck out the first two hitters in the top of the ninth, then walked Jorge Posada and allowed a single to Scott Brosius. Yankee second baseman Luis Sojo followed with a single up the middle, and center fielder Jay Payton's throw to the plate glanced off the Yankees' runner Jorge Posada, who scored to break the 2-2 tie and propel the Yankees to their first world championship of the 21st century.

Great Moments In Mets History

The New York Mets have almost 40 years worth of amazing history and we've spotlighted some of the most memorable moments.

The Mets celebrate their 1969 World Series victory.

October 15, 1969 – In Game 4 of the 1969 World Series, the Mets were clinging to a tenuous 1-0 lead over the powerful Baltimore Orioles. But the Orioles had runners on first and third with one out when Brooks Robinson smacked a sinking line drive to right center. Mets outfielder **Ron Swoboda** raced over, dove with his arm outstretched and made a tremendous sliding catch, snaring the ball just

All-time Mets great Tom Seaver.

inches above the ground. The tying run scored, but the catch saved the game for the Mets, who went on to win in the 10th inning.

April 22, 1970 and October 6, 1991 – On the night he was presented with the Cy Young Award for his masterful 1969 season, **Tom Seaver** threw one of the best games in baseball history. In front of a jubilant Shea Stadium crowd, "Tom Terrific" set a record by striking out 19 San Diego Padres. In 1991 (after Seaver's record had been broken by Roger Clemens), Mets ace **David Cone** duplicated Seaver's amazing feat by striking out 19 Philadelphia Phillies batters, en route to a league-leading 241 strikeouts that year.

October 25, 1986 – One of the strangest and most exciting World Series finishes happened with the Mets trailing the Red Sox 5-3 in the 10th inning of Game 6. With two outs, the Mets tied the game on three singles and a wild pitch. Now the Mets had the winning run at

Mookie Wilson (above) and a dejected Bill Buckner (right).

third, but the inning looked over when Mookie Wilson grounded a Bob Stanley pitch to first baseman Bill Buckner. But Buckner let the ball go under his glove for an error and Ray Knight scored from third to give the Mets the game and momentum heading into Game 7.

October 9, 1999 – The Mets' wild postseason run started in the first-round divisional series against the Arizona Diamondbacks. After blowing a two-run lead in the eighth inning, the Mets got a shot at redemption in the 10th inning with the game tied up 3-3.

Todd Pratt is surrounded by Mets teammates after his series-winning home run.

Backup catcher Todd Pratt hit a shot to dead center and the ball snuck over the wall just beyond the glove of leaping outfielder Steve Finley for a dramatic series-ending home run.

October 17, 1999 – In Game 5 of the N.L.C.S against the Atlanta Braves, the Mets were on the brink of elimination when the Braves took a one-run lead in the top of the 15th inning. In the bottom of the 15th, the Mets loaded the

Mets third baseman Robin Ventura.

bases, then Todd Pratt walked to force in the tying run. Then up came Robin Ventura who drilled a pitch over the right-field fence for a grand slam to win the game. The hit was later changed to a single because Ventura never reached second base in the chaos that followed.

Game 3 hero Benny Agbayani.

October 7, 2000 – Shea Stadium fans enjoyed yet another postseason marathon when the Mets took on the Giants in the National League Division Series. With the series tied 1-1 in Game 3, the two teams were deadlocked at two runs each going into the bottom of the 13th inning. Then Mets outfielder Benny Agbayani stepped up and belted a one-out, game-winning homer into the left field stands, giving the Mets a crucial 2-1 series lead.

Yankees Single-Season Records

Batting

Highest Batting Average:

Babe Ruth, 1923 393

Most Home Runs:

Roger Maris, 1961 61

Most RBI:

Lou Gehrig, 1931 184

Most Runs:

Babe Ruth, 1921 177

Most Hits:

Don Mattingly, 1986 238

Most Consecutive Games Hitting Safely:

Joe DiMaggio, 1941 56

Most Doubles:

Don Mattingly, 1986 53

Most Triples:

Earle Combs, 1927 23

Most Total Bases:

Babe Ruth, 1921 457

Babe Ruth, the leader in five batting categories.

Lou Gehrig had 184 RBI in 1931.

Joe DiMaggio's 56-game hitting streak is a major league record.

Corbis
Earle Combs hit 23 triples in 1927.

Corbis
Spud Chandler had a sparkling 1.64 ERA in 1943.

AP/WWP
Ron Guidry struck out 248 batters in the 1978 season.

Yankees Single-Season Records, cont.

Batting, cont.

Highest Slugging Percentage:

Babe Ruth, 1920 847

Most Bases On Balls:

Babe Ruth, 1923 170

Most Stolen Bases:

Rickey Henderson, 1988 93

Pitching

Most Wins:

Jack Chesbro, 1904 41

Lowest ERA:

Spud Chandler, 1943 . . . . . 1.64

Most Innings Pitched:

Jack Chesbro, 1904 454

Most Strikeouts:

Ron Guidry, 1978 248

Most Saves:

Dave Righetti, 1986 46

Most Complete Games:

Jack Chesbro, 1904 48

Mets Single-Season Records

Batting

Highest Batting Average:

John Olerud, 1998 354

Most Home Runs:

Todd Hundley, 1996 41

Most RBI:

Mike Piazza, 1999 124

Most Runs:

Edgardo Alfonzo, 1999 123

Most Hits:

Lance Johnson, 1996 227

Most Consecutive Games
Hitting Safely:

Hubie Brooks, 1984 24

Mike Piazza, 1999 24

Most Doubles:

Bernard Gilkey, 1996 44

Most Triples:

Lance Johnson, 1996 21

Most Total Bases:

Lance Johnson, 1996 327

John Olerud had a .354 batting average for the Mets in 1998.

Todd Hundley bashed a club-record 41 home runs in 1996.

Mike Piazza has started to make his mark on the Mets record book.

AP/WWP

Roger Cedeno stole 66 bases as a rookie in 1999.

AP/WWP

Tom Seaver, the leader in four pitching categories.

AP/WWP

Armando Benitez had 41 saves in 2000.

Mets Single–Season Records, cont.

Batting, cont.

Highest Slugging Percentage:

Mike Piazza, 2000 614

Most Bases On Balls:

John Olerud, 1999 125

Most Stolen Bases:

Roger Cedeno, 1999 66

Pitching

Most Wins:

Tom Seaver, 1969 25

Lowest ERA:

Dwight Gooden, 1985 . . . . . 1.53

Most Innings Pitched:

Tom Seaver, 1970 291

Most Strikeouts:

Tom Seaver, 1971 289

Most Saves:

Armando Benitez, 2000 41

Most Complete Games:

Tom Seaver, 1971 21